Celebrate your life!

♡ Anita '08 aspen

Hope this inspires you
to enjoy your friends and family
like this book.

Elaine

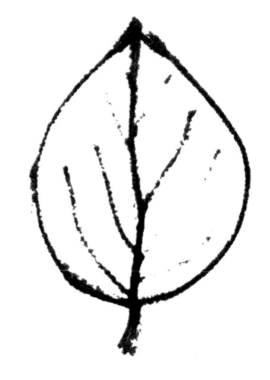

Thursdays with Mom & Michael

A DAUGHTER'S LOVING TRIBUTE
TO HER MOTHER'S WEEKLY
DINNER PARTIES
IN ASPEN

ISBN-13: 978-0-615-19296-3

PUBLISHER
Red Mountain Press
1055 St. Paul Place
Cincinnati, Ohio 45202
513.381.8696
DISTRIBUTOR
ARStudio@aol.com
www.AnitaRosenberg.com
RECIPES
Michael Rueggeberg
PHOTOGRAPHER
Karl Wolfgang
ART DIRECTOR AND LAYOUT ARTIST
Karl Wolfgang
GRAPHIC DESIGN AND TYPESETTING
words pictures colours graphic design

Printed in China

Thursdays with Mom & Michael

A DAUGHTER'S LOVING TRIBUTE
TO HER MOTHER'S WEEKLY
DINNER PARTIES
IN ASPEN

dedicated to
GRANDMA ANNE,
WHO LEFT THIS WORLD TOO SOON

by ANITA AND ELAINE ROSENBERG

with CHEF MICHAEL RUEGGEBERG

photography by KARL WOLFGANG

a celebration of life

I am dedicating **Thursdays with Mom &
Michael** to celebrate my life and to celebrate
the lives of other breast cancer survivors. As a
twenty-three-year breast cancer survivor, I want
to say thank you to life by donating all of my
royalties from this book to breast cancer research
through The Breast Cancer Research Foundation
founded by Evelyn Lauder. My hope is that our
children and grandchildren will never have to
worry about this threat to their lives. There are
many great tools that help with early detection,
but my wish is for prevention. I pray that my
small contribution can make a big difference to
help women of tomorrow.

- Elaine

$\mathcal{Y}$ou are holding in your hands a book about love and food. Food preparation in my mind has always been an act of affection for the cook and the persons dining. This energetic, colorful, and inspiring book is filled with creative ideas.

$\mathcal{M}$y most sincere thanks to Anita and Elaine Rosenberg for their generosity in supporting the excellent work of The Breast Cancer Research Foundation. Women everywhere will surely be grateful as well!

— Evelyn Lauder

FOUNDER AND CHAIRMAN
THE BREAST CANCER RESEARCH FOUNDATION

THE BREAST CANCER RESEARCH FOUNDATION
60 EAST 56TH STREET, 8TH FLOOR
NEW YORK, NY 10022
1-866-FIND-A-CURE (346-3228)
WWW.BCRFCURE.ORG

ALL AUTHOR ROYALTIES FROM
THE SALE OF THIS BOOK ARE DONATED
TO THE BREAST CANCER RESEARCH FOUNDATION

welco

me to
to

Thursdays

with

Mom &

Michael

you are invited

8

This book is a love letter to my mother, Elaine, the most talented and inspiring woman I have had the privilege to know and love. Throughout my life, my mom, my best friend, has impressed me with her artistic flair and her kind and caring nature. Our home has always been a magical place for our large family to gather and celebrate. In my eyes, she is the goddess of entertaining and her unique talent for blending a beautifully diverse crowd always gets rave reviews and keeps her guests coming back for more.

Although she loves throwing large events, my mother prefers small, intimate gatherings where people get a chance to really connect. In Aspen, she had this idea to host a weekly dinner party inviting ten new guests each week. Some folks would know each other and others wouldn't because she loves mixing it up. And that is when she met Michael Rueggeberg, the most sought after private chef in town. Thursdays were the only night Michael had available and that is how **Thursdays with Mom & Michael** became the hottest ticket in a very hot town!

When Michael takes center stage as star of the kitchen, the gang gathers around. Between him and his wife, Christine, who helps serve up those delectable dishes, they know just about everyone in Aspen. Born in Germany, Michael has traveled the globe perfecting his art, "Becoming a chef was the only job I ever wanted to do. Not a pilot. Not a race car driver. Only a chef!" His culinary credo of satisfying the senses while educating them at the same time fits in perfectly with my mother's philosophy of entertainment as fun and enlightenment.

Michael 2008

Elaine

DIOGENES HUN
FOR ONLY ONE
TRUTHFUL ARAB
CO

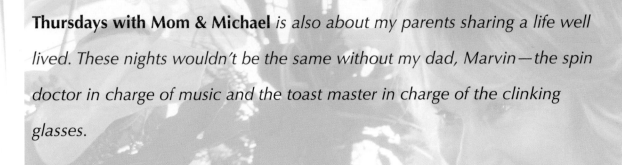

Thursdays with Mom & Michael *is also about my parents sharing a life well lived. These nights wouldn't be the same without my dad, Marvin—the spin doctor in charge of music and the toast master in charge of the clinking glasses.*

These weekly soirées link my parents in a virtually unbroken chain from the salons of George Sands and Coco Chanel in Paris, to the parlor of Katherine Brown, who came over the mountains with her family in 1880 and became the godmother of the Aspen party spirit. Just like my mom, Katherine invited Aspenites from all walks of life to gather around her table and share their differences, their similarities, and their experiences of high mountain life. It is in this tradition of community, fellowship, and healthy appetites that my mother throws her parties.

I offer these loving portraits of this season's **Thursdays with Mom & Michael** *to honor my mother's passion and artistry for entertaining, my father's sense of fun, and our family's tradition of enjoying a feast of the senses together, while restoring our spirits weekly with good food, good wine, and good company. Keep in mind that you don't need a party planner or a large budget, all you need is a resourceful imagination and some willing assistance. This is my invitation to you to be inspired to invent a weekly ritual of your own that celebrates your family and friends, old and new, just like we do in Aspen.*

Contents

A Taste
of Tuscany

Tuscany is one of my very favorite places. The countryside and the people are warm and relaxed. The first year I took my family to Italy was special because it was where I celebrated the end of my cancer treatments. It was a magical time of sailing to Sardinia and Portofino, viewing masterpieces in Venice, Rome and Florence, then visiting medieval castles and wine tasting throughout Tuscany and Chianti. To this day, those colors, smells, and sounds restore my spirit and rejuvenate my soul. For me, there is nowhere as life-affirming as Italy, so I've chosen to open this soirée season with a Taste of Tuscany, to share the spirit of that special time and place with the people that I love, right here in my own family dining room.

-Elaine

setting the table

My mother's world of tabletop is an organic process of mixing and matching, like an artist painting a masterpiece. Her table is her canvas and the end result is always a delightful surprise. Starting with the dishes and tablecloth as her base, she adds on from there. Hunting for the perfect artistic details might entail heading to downtown Aspen where she is sure to find the greatest entertaining accessories. For Tuscany, it was the rustic plates and chargers that she used as the cornerstone of her earthy settings. She picked up amazing Italian vases that put a twist on the usual centerpiece idea, and she filled them with ivy to reflect the vineyards and olive trees of the region.

For this theme, the color palette was crucial to re-creating the romance and passion of those La Dolce Vida nights. Warm terracotta and earth tones reminded her of the faded patinas from the churches while dozens of glowing candles on the table sparked that Italian spirit.

breaking the rules

My mother's design philosophy is **MORE is MORE**. She has never been one to follow the rules, and is not part of the less-is-more school of thought. Patterns, prints, and colors are her playground, and she has a reputation for creating a visual feast for the eyes with decor that someone else might not normally think to put together. To create a Tuscan tone, she juxtaposed pattern on pattern with paisley print napkins on top of festive Italian pottery and served burgundy colored Chianti in colorfully painted glass decanters normally used for flowers. Her philosophy is about following your own instincts and not being afraid to play and take risks. If you get excited and have fun creating your tablescape, your guests will enjoy it too!

planning the menu

Michael and my mother have been throwing parties together for so long there is an unspoken communication between them, and an abiding mutual respect. She never tells Michael what to cook, and he never tells her how to set a tabletop.

As soon as the theme is set, Michael begins researching the region so that he can present the purest and most authentic dishes possible. He learns that there is really no such thing as Italian cuisine as we generally think of it. Each area or province in Italy has its own unique and proud specialties. For instance, Roman cuisine uses a lot of sheeps' milk Pecorino cheese, and Piemonte and Lombardia grow their own unique varieties of rice, which are used to make their internationally renowned risottos. The north of Italy is the home of polenta. Emilia-Romagna is known for lasagna and tortellini. Naples is proud of their pizza, mozzarella, and pastries, and Tuscan cooking features white beans, meat, and unsalted bread. No matter where you go in Italy, every Italian table strives to present the very best of each season. Here's the very special Tuscan menu that Michael planned.

The best kitchens in Tuscany use only the freshest, seasonal produce. My menu for A Taste of Tuscany is planned while I am out shopping, so that I can see first-hand what is available. Finding fresher than fresh anything can be tricky in a town like Aspen, where everything must be flown or trucked in!

Michael

Menu

Antipasto

Bruschetta

Cured Italian Meats and Cheeses

Primo

Potato Gnocchi with Wild Spinach, Portobello Mushrooms,
Shallots, and White Truffle Oil

Roasted Butternut Squash Ravioli with Artichokes
and Brown Sage Butter

Secondo

Grilled Veal Chop with Soft Polenta, Garden Vegetables,
and Sun-Dried Tomato Sauce

Contorno

Tri-Colored Tomato Salad with Buffalo Mozzarella

Dolce

Baked Ricotta and Mascarpone Tart with Vanilla Bean
Ice Cream and White Cappuccino Biscotti

Special Drink of the Night

Peach Bellini

Roasted Butternut Squash Ravioli with Artichokes and Brown Sage Butter

Butternut Squash Purée

1 butternut squash (about 1 pound)
2 tablespoons softened butter, divided
Salt to taste
Pinch ground nutmeg
Pinch ground cinnamon

Halve the squash lengthwise and remove the seeds. Rub the insides with 1 tablespoon softened butter; season with salt and nutmeg. Place on a roasting pan, skin side down and bake in a preheated 350° F oven for 30 to 40 minutes or until fork tender. Remove the squash from the oven, scoop out the flesh and place in a food processor. Add remaining 2 tablespoons of butter and cinnamon. Purée until smooth.

Squash Ravioli

serves 6

11 tablespoons butter
4 tablespoons minced shallots
1 cup roasted butternut squash purée
1 cup fresh artichoke bottoms, cut in quarters
1 pint fresh teardrop tomatoes
Salt and fresh ground black pepper
3 tablespoons heavy cream
3 tablespoons grated Parmigiano-Reggiano cheese
Pinch nutmeg
Fresh pasta dough, buy at specialty grocery in wide ¼-inch ribbons
12 fresh sage leaves
1 tablespoon finely chopped fresh parsley leaves

In a large sauté pan, over medium heat, melt 1 tablespoon of the butter. Add the shallots and sauté for 1 minute. Add the squash purée and cook until the mixture is slightly dry, about 2 to 3 minutes. Season with salt and pepper. Stir in the cream and continue to cook for 2 minutes. Remove from heat and stir in 3 tablespoons cheese and nutmeg, season to taste with salt and pepper. Cool completely. Cut the pasta ribbons into 3-inch squares. Place 2 teaspoons of the filling in the center of each pasta square. Bring 1 corner of the square to the other, forming a triangle, and seal the pasta completely. Add the pasta to a pot of boiling, salted water. Cook until al dente, about 2 to 3 minutes or until the pasta floats and is pale in color. Remove the pasta from the water and drain well. Season the pasta with salt and pepper. In a medium sauté pan, heat 1 teaspoon butter and sauté the artichokes and teardrop tomatoes. Season to taste with salt and pepper, set aside and keep warm. In a large sauté pan, melt the remaining 8 tablespoons of butter. Add the sage to the butter and continue to cook until the butter starts to brown. Remove from the heat. Place the artichoke and tomato ragout in the center of each serving plate. Place two ravioli on top and spoon the butter sauce over the pasta. Sprinkle 2 ounces of cheese over each plate and garnish with parsley. Serve immediately.

Grilled Veal Chop with Soft Polenta, Garden Vegetables, and Sun-Dried Tomato Sauce

Veal Chop

serves 6

5 tablespoons extra-virgin olive oil
¼ cup dry red wine
1½ tablespoons chopped fresh rosemary or 2 teaspoons dried
2 large garlic cloves, pressed
½ teaspoon salt
½ teaspoon ground black pepper
6, 8-ounce veal rib chops, bone in (¾ to 1-inch thick)
Fresh rosemary sprigs
2 cups brown veal stock
½ cup sun-dried tomato, dehydrated in warm water, thinly sliced

Whisk oil, wine, rosemary, garlic, salt, and pepper and pour into a 13 x 9 x 2 inch glass baking dish. Add veal chops to the baking dish and turn the chops so that they are coated with the marinade. Let stand at room temperature 1 hour or refrigerate up to 4 hours, turning the veal occasionally. Prepare barbecue (medium-high heat) or preheat broiler. Remove chops from the marinade and shake off excess liquid. Season with salt and pepper and place on a lightly oiled grill. Grill or broil veal, about 4 minutes per side for medium-rare. Set aside and cover to keep the chops warm. For the sauce, heat up brown veal stock over low heat and bring to simmer. Pat dry the sun-dried tomatos and add to the sauce.

Soft Polenta

4 cups organic whole milk
4 cups organic chicken broth
2 cups polenta (coarse cornmeal)
Kosher salt and black pepper to taste
Pinch of nutmeg

To prepare the polenta, whisk 4 cups chicken broth, polenta, and salt in heavy large saucepan. Stir over medium heat until mixture comes to simmer. Gradually whisk in 4 cups of milk. Bring to boil, whisking the polenta often. Reduce heat to low; cover and cook until polenta is thick, soft, and creamy, stirring often, about 30 minutes. Set aside and keep warm.

Vegetables

12 each green asparagus, peeled
12 each white asparagus, peeled
12 each baby carrots
2 cups green beans
2 teaspoons parsley, finely chopped
2 teaspoons butter

To prepare the vegetables, bring salted water to a boil over high heat and blanch the vegetables until tender. In a medium sauté pan, heat butter over medium-high heat, add the vegetables and season to taste with salt, and finish with parsley. To assemble the dish, spoon the polenta in the center of the serving plate, arrange the vegetables on top of polenta and place the veal chop bone up. Spoon sun-dried tomato sauce over the veal chop and around the plate. Garnish with a rosemary sprig and serve immediately.

Tri-Colored Tomato Salad with Buffalo Mozzarella

Salad

serves 6

6 small balls mozzarella cheese
2 small yellow tomatoes
2 small red tomatoes
2 small orange tomatoes
12 large fresh basil leaves
3 tablespoons extra-virgin olive oil
4 cups arugula leaves
½ cup shaved Parmigiano-Reggiano cheese

Basil Vinaigrette

½ cup fresh basil leaves
½ cup extra-virgin olive oil
4 tablespoons balsamic vinegar
¼ tablespoon honey
Kosher salt and fresh ground black pepper

Blanch the basil leaves in boiling, salted water for about 30 seconds. Drain the leaves under cold, running water; drain well and dry on paper towels. Next, pulse the basil, honey, and balsamic vinegar in a food processor and then with the machine running, slowly add the olive oil, blending until smooth. This can be done up to two days ahead; store vinaigrette in the refrigerator and bring to room temperature before serving. To arrange the salad, toss the tomatoes with the mozzarella cheese, fresh basil, and extra-virgin olive oil and arrange on a platter. Toss the arugula leaves with the vinaigrette and on top of the tomatoes, sprinkle with shaved Parmigiano-Reggiano cheese and drizzle with extra vinaigrette.

Baked Ricotta and Mascarpone Tart with Vanilla Bean Ice Cream and White Cappuccino Biscotti

Pastry

serves 8

Uncooked pastry dough (buy at grocery and place inside 9-inch tart shell)

Slice very thin slivers of your pastry lengthwise and place slivers all around your tart mold, fitting them together as tightly as possible. Tie up the sides and cut off any excess pastry from the rim. Place in the freezer for one hour. For an uncooked filling, bake the tart 'blind' (without filling) for around 15 minutes on 350° F. This will cook the pastry all the way through, and give a light color to your pastry. Next, brush the inside with a little egg white and put it back in the oven for 30 seconds, to keep the pastry crisp.

Filling

7 ounces ricotta cheese
10 ounces mascarpone cheese
1 cup confectioners' sugar
3 oranges, zested (small peeling of orange skin)
1 seed from vanilla bean
2 whole eggs, separated
1 whole egg, beaten
3½ ounces white chocolate, roughly chopped
½ cup sliced almonds

To make the filling, turn the oven to 325° F. Whisk together the ricotta, mascarpone, sugar, orange zest, vanilla, and egg yolks until smooth and shiny. In a separate bowl, whisk egg whites until stiff. Fold egg whites gently into the mixture, and finally fold in the chocolate and almonds. Pour into a cooled tart pan. Lay about seven strips of pastry over the filling and then place seven strips of pastry the other way on top of them, creating a criss-cross pattern. Brush the pastry with the beaten egg and bake in preheated oven for 40-45 minutes. The tart should be served warm with vanilla bean ice cream, fresh strawberries, and fresh mint leaves.

Biscotti

1 box of white cappuccino biscotti (specialty food store)

An Evening
in Provence

France is a passion for me. My house is Country French and I love to set my table like a countryside picnic with blue, yellow, and white. For three summers our family stayed at an old olive mill that was converted into a rustic farmhouse in the hills of Vence. So every winter, even though we are many miles away from France, I treat my friends and family to that invigorating and liberating feeling of the French countryside, with a very special evening in Provence, right here in Aspen!

-Elaine

what is quimper anyway?

Since my mother's Aspen house is decorated in Country French, she knows how to bring that warm country feeling to the table. Quimper (pronounced "kem-pair") is a classic French pottery that comes from the town of Quimper. It is tin-glazed earthenware, with hand-painted scenes depicting life in Brittany, that has been in production since 1707. Her collection of old and new Quimper pottery started on our family trips to the South of France. Mixing and matching them is one of the fun things she likes to do.

41

the gallic rooster

(COQ GAULOIS) IS THE FRENCH NATIONAL EMBLEM

— and a clever motif for place cards and napkin rings.

When I was young, my culinary apprenticeship in Germany was all about learning the basics and how to cook and prepare French cuisine. We were taught that all famous chefs came from France so I learned about the strong emphasis on fresh ingredients such as olives, tomatoes, zucchini, eggplant, and lemons. One bite of this Provence menu and you will understand why "Provençal cuisine" has earned the nickname "la cuisine du soleil" (cuisine of the sun).

Michael

Menu

Appetizers

Blue Cheese Gougère

Vol au Vent

Country Bread with Three Kinds of Spreads

Main

French Onion Soup with Gruyère Garlic Bread

Filet of Sole with White Bean Purée and Provençal Artichokes

Spinach and Bacon Quiche with Organic Mesclun Herb Salad in a Hazelnut Vinaigrette

Roasted Chicken with Braised Vegetables and New Potatoes

Dessert

Sour Cherry Clafouti

Special Drink of the Night

Kir Royal

Spinach and Bacon Quiche with Organic Mesclun Herb Salad in a Hazelnut Vinaigrette

Spinach and Bacon Filling

serves 6-8

1, 9-inch pie form
6 ounces thick cut bacon, cut into narrow strips (or "lardons")
2 large eggs
2 large egg yolks
2 cups fresh spinach leaves, chopped
1¼ cups heavy whipping cream
Pinch freshly grated nutmeg
1 cup grated Gruyère cheese

In a medium skillet, cook the bacon until crisp and the fat is rendered, about 5 minutes. Remove with a slotted spoon and drain on paper towels. Discard the fat or reserve for another use. Arrange the bacon evenly over the bottom of the baked crust; layer the spinach over it. In a large bowl, beat the eggs, yolks, and whipping cream. Add the remaining ingredients and whisk to combine. Pour into the prepared crust and bake until the custard is golden, puffed, and slightly wiggly in the center, 30 to 35 minutes. Remove from the oven and let cool on a wire rack for 15 minutes before serving. Serve with organic mesclun salad.

Flaky Butter Crust

9-inch tart or pie crust
1¼ cups all-purpose flour
¼ teaspoon salt
7 tablespoons unsalted butter, chilled and cut into pieces
1 to 2 tablespoons ice water, or more as needed

To make the dough in a food processor, combine the flour, salt, and butter and process until the mixture resembles coarse crumbs, about 10 seconds. With the machine running, add the ice water through the feed tube and pulse quickly 5 or 6 times, or until the dough comes together and starts to pull away from the sides of the container. Kneed the dough into a ball, flatten it into a disk, and wrap in plastic wrap. Refrigerate for at least 1 hour. On a lightly floured surface, roll out the dough to an 11-inch circle. Fit into a 9-inch pie form with a removable bottom and trim the edges. (Alternatively, a 9-inch pie pan can be used.) Refrigerate for at least 30 minutes. Preheat the oven to 375°F. Line the pastry with parchment paper and fill with pie weights or dried beans. Bake until the crust is set, 12 to 14 minutes. Remove the paper and weights and bake until golden brown, 8 to 10 minutes. Remove from the oven and cool on a wire rack.

Organic Mesclun Herb Salad in a Hazelnut Vinaigrette

¼ cup apple cider vinegar

2 teaspoons dark brown sugar, optional

1 teaspoon Dijon mustard

1 tablespoon chopped garlic

Salt and fresh black pepper to taste

1 teaspoon, fresh chives, cut ½-inch long

1 teaspoon fresh tarragon leaves, picked

1 teaspoon fresh flat leaf parsley, picked

1 teaspoon fresh chervil, picked

¾ cup hazelnut oil

3 cups mesclun salad mix, for accompaniment

In a medium mixing bowl, whisk the vinegar with the mustard, sugar, garlic, salt, and pepper until sugar and salt dissolves. Then slowly whisk in the oil until emulsified, whisking constantly, adjust the seasonings. Toss a few tablespoons of the vinaigrette with the salad herb mix and serve immediately. If not using dressing right away, cover and refrigerate, whisking or shaking again before use.

Roasted Chicken with Braised Vegetables and New Potatoes

Roasted Chicken

serves 6

2 three-pound free range whole chickens
4 garlic cloves, peeled
2 sprigs fresh thyme
2 fresh oranges, washed, cut in half

Pull out the two pockets of fat from inside the body cavity and reserve 2 tablespoons for the chicken glaze. Cut off the wing tips and neck and coarsely chop. Preheat the oven 350° F. Cut the herb butter into 3-inch pieces. Gently work your hands between the skin and flesh of the chicken, works well with slightly oiled hands. Slide the herb butter sheets under the skin and then massage the chicken with your hands so that the butter softens and moves over the chicken flesh. Season inside and outside with salt and black pepper. Add the thyme, rosemary, garlic, and orange into the cavity. Truss the chickens and place in a roasting pan. Roast, basting often, for about 1 hour, until the skin is crispy and golden brown. To make sure the chicken is cooked, the juices should run clearly when the thigh is pierced. Transfer the chicken to a wired roasting rack and rest for at least 10 minutes. Before serving, remove the herbs, garlic, and oranges, skim off the fat from the juices and add the juices to the chicken glaze.

Chicken Glaze

2 tablespoons chicken fat (reserved from chicken)
2 small garlic cloves, peeled
2 shallots, peeled, chopped
1 sprig fresh thyme
1 sprig fresh rosemary
2-3 cups chicken stock

Coarsely chop the chicken fat and place in a small saucepan, heat over medium heat until it melts. Add the wing tips and neck, cook until browned. Pour off excess fat and stir in the shallot, garlic, thyme, and rosemary and pour in the chicken stock to cover. Bring to a boil, reduce heat, and reduce until syrupy. Strain and set aside.

Herb Butter

1½ sticks unsalted butter, softened
½ bunch each: fresh parsley, tarragon, chives, thyme (all stems removed and finely chopped)
Salt and fresh black pepper
Pinch cayenne pepper

While the chicken glaze is reducing, make the herb butter. In a medium bowl, mix the softened butter and chopped herbs. Season to taste with salt, pepper, and cayenne pepper. Place the herb butter on plastic wrap and spread evenly with a spatula about ⅛-inch thick. Cover with another sheet of plastic and cool until firm.

Braised Vegetables

5 tablespoons olive oil
¼ pound pearl onions, peeled
¼ pound cippolini onions, peeled
¼ pound carrots, peeled and cut in half
¼ pound celery root, peeled and cut in ½-inch pieces
¼ pound turnips, peeled and cut in ½-inch pieces
1¼ pound small new potatoes, scrubbed
1 tablespoon sugar
3 tablespoons unsalted butter
1 sprig fresh thyme, finely chopped
1 sprig fresh rosemary
Salt and fresh black pepper

While the chicken is roasting, prepare the vegetables. Heat 2 tablespoons of the oil in a large skillet, add the new potatoes, stir to coat with the oil, and season with salt. Cook over medium-high heat until the potatoes are golden brown and tender, shaking the pan often. Add the fresh rosemary and keep warm. In the meantime, in another large skillet, heat 2 tablespoons olive oil, add the carrots, celery, and turnips, stir to coat with the oil, and season with salt and black pepper. Cook over medium-high heat until the vegetables are caramelized and tender, shaking the pan often. Combine with the potatoes. In a small skillet, combine the pearl onions and cippolini onions with 2 tablespoons butter and the sugar. Add enough water to cover and season with salt. Bring to a simmer until the liquid has reduced to golden brown and the onions are tender, 10-12 minutes. Add the thyme and roll the onions in the glaze to coat. To serve, add the remaining butter and the chicken glaze to the vegetables, bring to a simmer. Remove the trussing strings. Carve the chicken into 6 portions, place the chicken in the center of a dinner plate and surround the chicken with the vegetables, potatoes, and onions. Drizzle with the chicken-vegetable liquid and serve.

Sour Cherry Clafouti

Clafouti

serves 6

¼ cup plus 3 tablespoons sugar
¾ pound sour cherries, halved and pitted
¾ cup milk
¾ cup light cream
¾ cup flour
2 eggs
1 egg yolk
⅓ teaspoon salt
1 fresh vanilla bean, scraped
Vanilla sugar, for sprinkling

Preheat oven to 400° F and butter the individual baking forms well. Sprinkle the forms with 3 tablespoons of sugar and distribute the cherries over the sugar. In a blender, blend the milk, light cream, flour, eggs, egg yolk, and salt for 2 minutes. Add the ¼ cup sugar and the scraped vanilla bean. Blend the mixture for a few seconds and pour it over the cherries. Bake the clafouti in the middle of the oven for about 30 minutes or until puffed and golden. Dust the clafouti with vanilla sugar and serve with the vanilla sauce and vanilla ice cream.

Vanilla Sauce

4 egg yolks, lightly beaten
½ cup sugar
2 cups heavy whipping cream
1 fresh vanilla bean, scraped

While the clafouti is baking, prepare the vanilla sauce. Beat the egg yolks and sugar together with a wire whisk or a rotary or electric beater for 3 or 4 minutes, or until the yolks are thick and pale yellow. Scrape the vanilla bean, add to the cream, and bring cream to a boil in a heavy 2- to 3-quart saucepan. Let sit for 20 minutes to get the flavor from the vanilla. Then, beating constantly with a whisk, pour the cream in a thin stream over the yolks. Pour the mixture back into the saucepan and cook over low heat, stirring constantly with a spoon, until the sauce is thick enough to coat the spoon lightly. Do not let the sauce come to a boil or it may curdle. Remove the pan from the heat and strain through a fine mesh strainer.

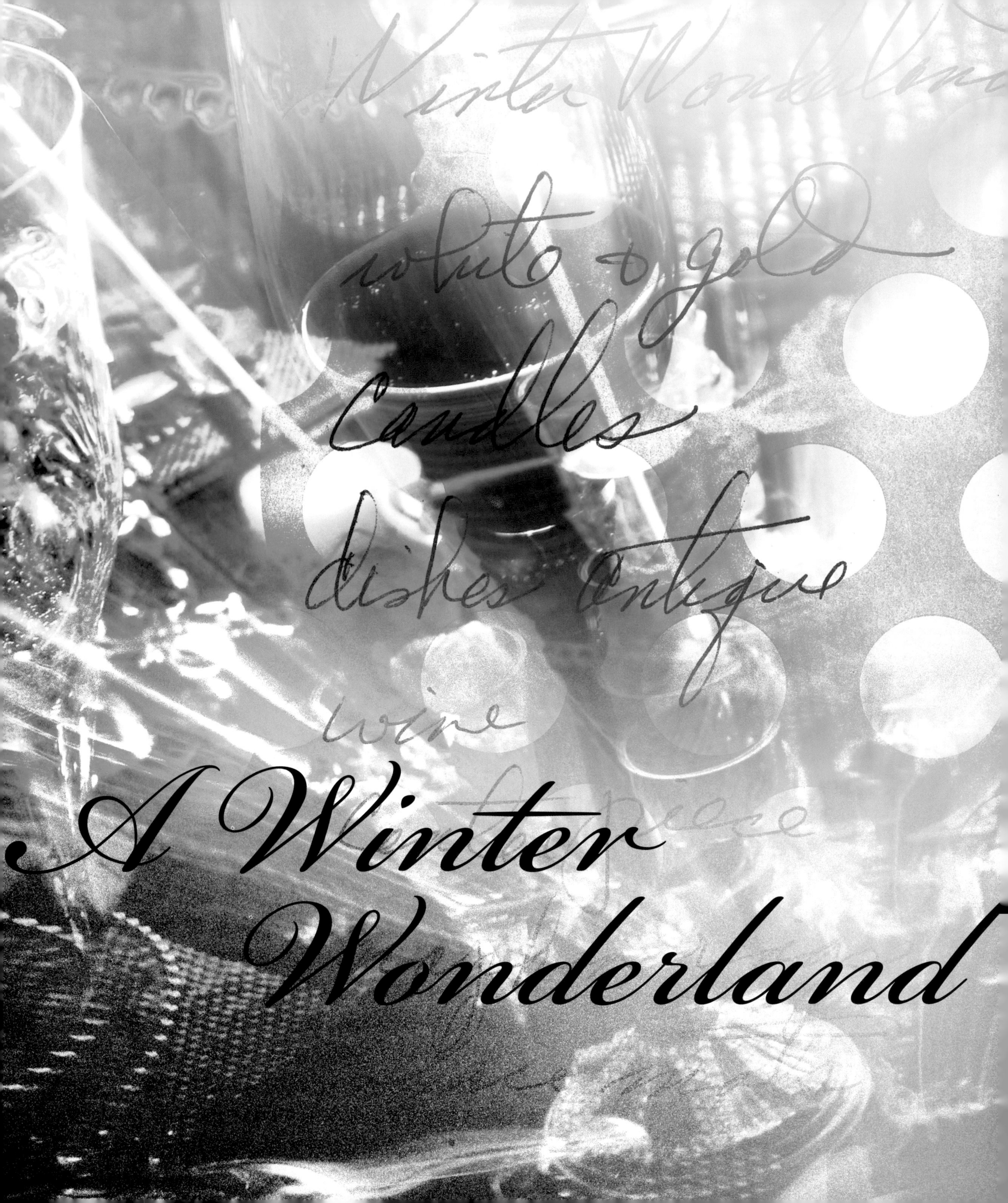
Winter Wonderland
white & gold
candles
dishes antique
wine
A Winter Wonderland

Winter Wonderland is about celebrating my friends and family during the holidays. This is the time of year I cherish most because my children, grandchildren, and friends are all in town, so it's a very social occasion. We all get to dress with a little glitz and glamour, and I always take the opportunity to set the stage with my most dramatic tabletops of the season. These nights are all about living in the here and now, giving thanks for the many blessings in our lives, most importantly, each other!

-Elaine

CHARGE IT!

Elaine's memory closet

Chargers are those large decorative plates you set your dishes on. They are like a frame for your plate, and create an integrated and elegant look when your guests sit down at the table. There is a lovely juxtaposition to layering rich textures of patterns and designs. My mother chose a white and gold theme for Winter Wonderland because it looks and feels rich and royal. The point is to capture the spirit of the season with sparkle. When you add the classy touch of chargers it creates elegance.

When snow falls in Aspen and the ski season begins, it brings back memories of when I worked in the European Alps. This is where I learned both modern and traditional ways of preparing hearty winter fare. With this Winter Wonderland menu I wanted to present an array of taste sensations from the mountain regions of Germany, Switzerland, Austria, and Italy, showing that although each cuisine is distinctive they also provide a smooth transition for the palate.

Michael

Menu

Appetizers

Gravlox on Blue Potato Chips

Roasted Asparagus Wrapped in Prosciutto

Main

Roasted Red Beet Carpaccio with Organic Mixed Greens and

Blue Cheese Crumbles in a Pear Vinaigrette

Sun-Dried Tomato Risotto with Crispy Seared Scallops in Tomato Butter

Lobster Corn Bisque

Pan-Seared Venison in Blackberry Sauce with Hazelnut Spaetzle

Dessert

Marbled Chocolate Cake in French Raspberry Sauce

Special Drink of the Night

Valrhona Hot Chocolate with Spiced Rum

Roasted Red Beet Carpaccio with Organic Mixed Greens and Blue Cheese Crumbles in a Pear Vinaigrette

Beets

12 medium red beets or 6 large beets (3 pounds, with greens, trimmed)
8 cups of organic greens
3 tablespoons blue cheese crumbles

Preheat oven to 400°F. Tightly wrap beets in double layers of foil to make 3 packages (2 large beets or 4 medium per package) and roast on a baking sheet in middle of oven until tender, 1¼ to 1½ hours. Cool in foil packages (the steam makes beets easier to peel) about 30 minutes. Peel and slice very thin.

Pear Vinaigrette

4 teaspoons pear vinegar
1 teaspoon shallots, minced
½ teaspoon Dijon mustard
¼ cup canola oil
¼ cup extra-virgin olive oil
½ teaspoon salt
¼ teaspoon fresh ground black pepper

To make the vinaigrette, combine the vinegar, mustard, and minced shallots. Season with salt and fresh black pepper. Slowly whisk in the oils until emulsified. Adjust seasoning. To arrange the salad, brush a plate with some of the pear vinaigrette. Arrange the sliced beet onto the vinaigrette, brush with more pear vinaigrette, season with fresh black pepper. In a medium bowl toss the organic greens with the pear vinaigrette, season with salt and pepper and place on top of the sliced beets; sprinkle with blue cheese crumbles.

Sun-Dried Tomato Risotto with Crispy Seared Scallops in Tomato Butter

Seared Scallops

serves 6

1½ pounds fresh sea scallops, approximately 12
2 teaspoons unsalted butter
2 teaspoons olive oil
Salt and fresh black pepper

Remove the small side muscle from the scallops, rinse under cold water, and thoroughly pat dry. Add the butter and oil to a 12 to 14-inch sauté pan on high heat. Salt and pepper the scallops. Once the fat begins to smoke, gently add the scallops, making sure they are not touching each other. Sear the scallops for 1½ minutes on each side. The scallops should have a quarter-inch golden crust on each side while still being translucent in the center.

Sun-Dried Tomato Risotto

¼ cup butter
3 tablespoons olive oil
2 tablespoons shallots, minced
12 sun-dried tomatoes, julienned
1 cup Arborio rice
4½ cups vegetable stock
8 ounces Portobello mushrooms, sliced
Salt and fresh ground pepper
2 ounces fresh Parmesan cheese
Fresh basil, finely chopped to garnish

Heat butter and 1 tablespoon oil in a medium saucepot. Add the shallots and cook, stirring occasionally, 5 minutes, or until soft. Add Arborio rice and cook, stirring, 1 minute. Stir in about one-third of stock and simmer, stirring occasionally, until most of the liquid has been absorbed. Add half of the remaining stock and simmer, stirring occasionally. Meanwhile, heat 2 tablespoons olive oil in a medium skillet. Add Portobello mushrooms and sauté for about 2-3 minutes, until tender. Season with salt and black pepper. When most of the liquid has been absorbed, stir in remaining stock and simmer until all liquid has been absorbed and rice is tender and creamy. Add sun-dried tomatoes and mushrooms and cook 1 or 2 minutes. Using a vegetable peeler, shave curls of Parmesan cheese over risotto, sprinkle with basil. Set the scallops on top and spoon the sauce around to serve.

Tomato Butter Sauce

2 cups store-bought marinara sauce
¼ cup dry white wine
½ cup heavy whipping cream
2 tablespoons shallots
2 sprigs fresh basil
2 tablespoons butter
Salt and fresh black pepper

In a medium saucepot, heat the butter, add the shallots, and sauté for about 1-2 minutes. Deglaze with white wine and reduce to half. Add the heavy whipping cream and reduce by ⅓. Add the marinara sauce, fresh basil, and bring to a simmer on medium heat. Simmer for 8-10 minutes. Transfer to blender and blend until smooth. Strain through a mesh strainer, season to taste with salt and pepper and keep warm. Before serving, whisk in remaining butter.

Lobster Corn Bisque

serves 8-10

2, 1-pound lobsters
6 ears fresh sweet corn
½ cup yellow onions, peeled and cut into 1-inch pieces
½ cup leeks, white parts only, washed and cut into 1-inch pieces
½ cup carrots, peeled and cut into 1-inch pieces
2 tablespoons extra-virgin olive oil
3 fresh bay leaves, or 2 dried
8 sprigs fresh thyme
1 tablespoon black peppercorns
Salt and fresh ground black pepper
1½ cups heavy cream
2 large Yukon Gold potatoes, peeled and cut into ¼-inch cubes
1 onion, chopped
2 teaspoons butter
2 tablespoons clarified butter
4 teaspoons chervil leaves
1 teaspoon chervil finely chopped

Lobster

Cook the lobsters in boiling, salted water for 3 to 4 minutes, or until slightly underdone. Remove from water and let cool slightly. Remove lobster meat from the shells, reserving the meat and the shells. Coarsely chop the lobster meat.

Corn

Remove husks from the corn and cut kernels off the cobs. Reserve the corn, cobs, and half of the husks.

Bisque

In a medium stockpot, heat up the olive oil over medium-high heat. Add the onions, leeks and carrots and sauté for about 8 minutes until caramelized. Place the lobster shells, corncobs, husks, bay leaves, thyme sprigs, and peppercorns into the stockpot and caramelize for another 8 minutes. Add enough water to barely cover. Simmer for 45 minutes, then strain through a fine mesh sieve, discarding the solids. Place the broth in a large saucepan and simmer over medium heat for 45 minutes, or until reduced to 1½ quarts. Season to taste with salt and pepper.

Pan-Seared Venison in Blackberry Sauce

Venison

serves 6

6 (6-ounce) venison loins
5 tablespoons olive oil
1 teaspoon black peppercorns
1 teaspoon juniper berries
1 teaspoon fennel seeds
1 teaspoon dried or fresh thyme leaves
2 sprigs fresh thyme
1 sprig fresh rosemary
1 fresh garlic clove
Salt and fresh black pepper
2 cups fresh Brussels sprouts
2 cups fresh green beans
1 teaspoon butter
Salt and fresh black pepper
Pinch of white sugar

In a spice grinder or food processor, grind the peppercorns, juniper berries, fennel seeds, and thyme together. Mix with 4 tablespoons of the olive oil and rub on the venison. Cover and let stand in the refrigerator for 4 to 6 hours. Remove the venison from the refrigerator one hour before cooking to come to room temperature. Heat a thick, ovenproof skillet until quite hot. Add just enough oil to coat bottom. Season venison liberally with salt and pepper. Place in skillet and brown on one side. Turn venison over and place skillet in oven to finish cooking. Add the thyme, rosemary, and garlic. Cook venison to medium rare, about 6 minutes, or until an instant read thermometer registers 135° F. Remove the outside leaves form the Brussels sprouts and trim the end of the beans. In a medium stockpot, bring water to a boil and season heavily with salt. Blanch the vegetables separately until cooked through, but still tender. Cut the cooked Brussels sprouts in half. In a medium skillet heat up the butter over medium-high heat, add the vegetables, and season with salt and sugar and lightly caramelize.

Blackberry Sauce

2 pints fresh blackberries, reserve 1 pint for garnish
½ tablespoon diced shallots
2 juniper berries
½ bay leaf
¼ cup red wine vinegar
¼ cup sugar
¼ cup water
½ cup demi-glace (brown veal stock)

Place all ingredients in a heavy saucepan and simmer until very soft. Push through a mesh strainer to remove pulp. Add demi-glace and keep warm. Before serving add the remaining blackberries and bring to simmer, do not boil. Slice the venison loin against the grain and place on the dish. Garnish with blackberries and finish with the sauce.

Marbled Chocolate Cake in Fresh Raspberry Sauce

Chocolate Cake

make in 10-inch tube pan

1 cup unsalted butter (2 sticks), plus more for the pan

2 cups sugar

4 large eggs

1 cup milk

1 fresh vanilla bean, scraped (or 1 tablespoon vanilla extract)

2½ cups flour, plus more for the pan

2 teaspoons baking powder

Pinch salt

3 tablespoons cocoa powder, sifted

½ cup marzipan paste

Butter and flour a straight-walled 10-inch tube pan. Preheat the oven to 350° F. In a standing mixer fitted with the paddle attachment, cream the butter until light and fluffy. Add the sugar and continue to mix well. Add the eggs one at a time and beat until incorporated. In a bowl, whisk together the milk and vanilla. In another bowl, whisk together the flour, baking powder, and salt. Reduce mixer to low speed. Alternately add the flour and milk mixture until a smooth batter is formed. Continue mixing for 2-3 minutes. Transfer ⅓ of the batter to a bowl and whisk in the cocoa powder. Stir the marzipan paste into the remaining batter. Pour the white batter into the pan, then spoon the chocolate batter around. Run a fork or knife through the batter, cutting the batters together to create a marbled effect. Do not stir. Bake until a toothpick inserted into the middle of the cake comes out clean, about 1 hour 15 minutes. Let the cake cool in the pan. Invert the cake onto a stand or plate, slice, and serve.

Fresh Raspberry Sauce

2 cups fresh or frozen raspberries (thaw before using)

1 teaspoon powdered sugar

2 fresh mint leaves

Purée raspberries and sugar in a blender until smooth. Strain through a fine mesh strainer. The sauce can be served hot or cold. To serve hot, transfer sauce to a small saucepan and bring to a simmer over medium heat. Remove from the heat and let cool for 20 minutes before serving with ice cream.

Pearls of Asia

*E*very year, I throw the Pearls of Asia party for my daughter, Anita, who has traveled extensively in this part of the world, and whose knowledge of Asian cultures shines as brightly as my three wise men. This year, she sent me Lucky Cats from Chinatown in Los Angeles to give as parting gifts. They are traditional Japanese charms that bring fortunate blessings, so I wanted my guests to leave with a bit of good luck. I love the stories that my blue willow plates tell of fated lovers, and my friends enjoy the exotic décor and experimenting with unfamiliar flavors and taste combinations. Plus, I get a chance to entertain in my Chinese cheongsam pantsuit from Shanghai Tang!

-Elaine

how lucky cats got lucky

The legend of the Lucky Cat grew out of the Maneki Neko (招き猫, literally "Beckoning Cat"; also known as Welcoming Cat, Lucky Cat, or Fortune Cat.) Japanese merchants are very superstitious, and they always keep some type of lucky charm at either the front or back door of their stores to attract good luck and prosperity. I learned first-hand about Lucky Cats on my trips to Asia. The key to these feline figurines is that they come in pairs. When the right paw is raised it attracts money and new business, while the left paw raised wards off negative energy and evil. For the Pearls of Asia party, these charmers made the perfect gift to give to parting guests as a rememberance of the evening.

Michael Rüggeberg
Chef de Cuisine

A few years ago, I traveled extensively throughout Asia and spent a month in Thailand, Malaysia, Singapore, Bali, and Japan. As a westerner, I fell in love with the unfamiliar flavors and taste combinations of Asian cuisine so I always enjoy creating a rich, diverse, and intriguing menu that honors the wide variety of Oriental cooking styles.

Michael

87

Menu

Appetizers

Ahi Tuna Parfait in Sweet Chili Vinaigrette

Sesame Chicken Satay

Chicken Spring Rolls

Crispy Shrimp Tempura with Sweet and Sour Sauce

Pork Pot Stickers

Main

Roasted Sweet Corn and Lemon Grass Soup with Lobster Fennel Salad

Vegetable Pad Thai

Grilled Teriyaki Beef Tenderloin with Wasabi Mashed Potatoes
and Asian Ratatouille

Dessert

Pineapple Coconut Cake

Special Drink of the Night

Daiginjo-shu Sake Martini

Roasted Sweet Corn and Lemon Grass Soup with Lobster Fennel Salad

Soup

serves 8-10

2 tablespoons canola oil
3 cups white onions, roughly chopped
2 tablespoons ginger, finely chopped
2 cups lemon grass, white parts only
8 cups corn kernels, fresh plus cobs
8 cups vegetable stock, or low sodium canned broth
Salt and fresh black pepper to taste

Heat up a medium-size pot over medium heat. Add the oil and swirl to coat the bottom. Add the onions, ginger, and lemon grass and sauté for about 8 minutes. Add the corn and the cobs and sauté for another eight minutes until the corn is slightly caramelized. Add the vegetable stock and bring to a boil. Reduce heat and simmer for about 30-40 minutes until the corn is soft. Discard the cob and transfer soup to the food processor and blend until puréed and of smooth consistency. Strain through a fine chinoise and season to taste. Keep warm until ready to be served.

Lobster Fennel Salad

½ pound fresh lobster, cooked (1 large tail), cut in ½-inch pieces
½ cup fennel bulb, finely shaved
¼ cup chives, cut ½-inch long
1 tablespoon extra-virgin olive oil
1 tablespoon canola oil
Juice of 1 lemon
1 tablespoon sesame oil
Salt and fresh black pepper to taste

In a medium bowl, combine the lobster meat, shaved fennel, and chives, and mix with the oils and lemon juice and season to taste. Arrange 1 tablespoon of the salad in the center of a soup bowl. Fill the soup bowl with the soup and drizzle some sesame oil around.

Vegetable Pad Thai

serves 6 as a noodle course or 3 as a main course

10 ounces Thai rice noodles
¼ cup tamarind paste
¼ cup warm water
4 ounces fried tofu
6 tablespoons roasted unsalted peanuts
3 tablespoons fish sauce
2 tablespoons sugar
2 tablespoons lime juice
½ cup vegetable oil
1 cup coconut milk, unsweetened
1 teaspoon garlic, finely chopped
2 eggs
1½ cups bean sprouts
2 green onion stems, cut into 1-inch pieces
Fresh cilantro leaves
1 lime, cut into wedges

Soak noodles in plenty of cold water for at least 1 hour. Combine tamarind paste with a ¼ cup warm water in a small bowl and let soak for at least 15 minutes. Slice the fried tofu into ¾-inch cubes and set aside. Blend or process peanuts into coarse meal. Mash the tamarind paste and its water in a medium mixing bowl and transfer the mud-like mixture to a strainer set into a bowl. Mash and push with a spoon, forcing liquid to strain into the bowl. Scrape off the juice that clings to the underside of the strainer. You will have about 5 tablespoons of tamarind juice. Add fish sauce, sugar, and lime juice. Beat the mix thouroughly and reserve. Discard the solids left in the strainer. Heat oil in a wok (or large frying pan) until it is just about to smoke. Add garlic and stir, letting it cook for about 30 seconds. Add tofu and stir-fry for one more minute. Crack eggs into wok and let them fry without breaking them up for 1-2 minutes. While eggs cook, quickly drain the noodles and then add to the wok, giving them a quick fold, stir-frying for 1 minute from the bottom up. Add reserved tamarind juice, coconut milk, and continue stir-frying, mixing everything together for 1-2 minutes. Your noodles will have expaded to twice their original volume and softened up to al dente. Add about ⅔ of the reserved ground peanuts and stir. Add about ⅔ of the bean sprouts and all the green onion pieces. Stir fry for 30 seconds and take off heat. Transfer noodles to a serving dish and sprinkle with the rest of the ground peanuts, the rest of the sprouts, and fresh cilantro leaves. Place a couple of lime wedges on the side and serve immediately.

Grilled Teriyaki Beef Tenderloin with Wasabi Mashed Potatoes and Asian Ratatouille

Teriyaki Beef

serves 6

1½ cups soy sauce
1 tablespoon cilantro
Juice and zest of 1 orange
Juice and zest of 1 lime
3 tablespoons brown sugar
4 garlic cloves, peeled, left whole
1 tablespoon fresh ginger, finely chopped
1 tablespoon white sesame seeds
6 beef tenderloins (about 6 ounces, preferably center cut)

To make the teriyaki marinade, combine the soy sauce, orange juice, lime juice, and zest with ginger, brown sugar, garlic, and cilantro in a medium pan. Bring to a boil over high heat, then reduce heat and simmer to syrupy consistency. About 15 minutes. Remove from heat. Stir in the sesame seeds and cool. Transfer to a baking dish and add the beef, turn to coat and marinate for at least 1 hour. Prepare outdoor grill, spray with non-stick cooking spray. Grill the beef over high heat, turning once until the beef is slightly charred, about 4 minutes each side. Brush with remaining sauce as it cooks. Remove from grill and set aside to rest.

Wasabi Mashed Potatoes

1 cup spinach leaves
1 cup fresh watercress
2 pounds baking potatoes, like russets, peeled and quartered
1 cup heavy cream, heated
4 ounces butter, cut into pieces
1 tablespoon wasabi paste
Salt and fresh ground black pepper

In a blender or food processor, process the spinach and watercress to a fine purée. Pass through a tamis or strainer. Reserve. Cook the potatoes in salted, boiling water until done. Pass through a ricer. Whisk in hot heavy cream and butter, one small piece at a time. Just before serving, stir in wasabi paste and purée of spinach and watercress. Stir until well incorporated. Season to taste with salt and pepper.

Asian Ratatouille

2 cups red bell peppers, cut into wedges
2 cups zucchini, cut into finger-sized sticks
2 cups broccoli roses, blanched in boiling, salted water
1 cup sesame oil
1 tablespoon fresh cilantro, finely chopped
Salt and fresh ground black pepper to taste

In a medium sauté pan, heat up sesame oil, add the peppers and zucchini and sauté until caramelized from all sides. Season to taste with salt and black pepper. Add the cilantro and remove from heat.

To assemble, place a wasabi mashed potato in the center of serving plate, arrange the vegetables on top of the mashed potatoes. Place the tenderloin on top of the vegetables and spoon remaining sauce over it.

Pineapple Coconut Cake

Cake

1 cup butter, softened

2 cups granulated sugar

4 large eggs

3 cups sifted cake flour

1 tablespoon baking powder

¼ teaspoon salt

1 cup milk

1 teaspoon vanilla extract

1 teaspoon almond extract

2 cups grated coconut

Preheat the oven to 350° F. Grease and flour a 9-inch round cake pan; set aside. Cream butter; gradually add sugar, beating well at medium speed in an electric mixer. Add eggs, one at a time, beating well after each addition. Combine flour, baking powder, and salt; add to creamed mixture alternately with milk, beginning and ending with flour mixture. Mix after each addition. Stir in extracts. Pour batter into prepared cake pans and bake in preheated oven for 25 to 30 minutes or until a toothpick inserted in center comes out clean. Cool in pans 10 minutes; remove from pans and cool completely on wire racks. Cut the cake in three layers. Spread 1 cake layer with half of the pineapple filling. Sprinkle ⅓ cup grated coconuts over filling. Repeat procedure with second layer. Makes one 3-layer cake.

Pineapple Filling

1 cup granulated sugar

3 tablespoons all-purpose flour

2 large eggs, beaten

1 (8-ounce) can crushed pineapple, undrained

2 tablespoons lemon juice

1 tablespoon butter

1 teaspoon vanilla extract

Combine sugar and flour in a small saucepan; add remaining ingredients. Cook over medium heat, stirring constantly, until thickened, about 2 minutes. Makes about 1⅓ cups filling.

Coconut Frosting

1½ cups granulated sugar

1¼ tablespoon cold water

2 large egg whites

1 tablespoon light corn syrup

Dash of salt

1 teaspoon vanilla extract

2 tablespoons grated coconut

Combine all ingredients except vanilla and coconut in the top of a large double boiler. Beat at low speed in an electric mixer 30 seconds or until blended. Place over boiling water; beat constantly at high speed 7 minutes or until stiff peaks form. Remove from heat. Add vanilla and coconut. Beat 2 minutes or until frosting is thick enough to spread. Makes 4¼ cups of frosting. Serve with pineapple coconut ice cream and fresh raspberries.

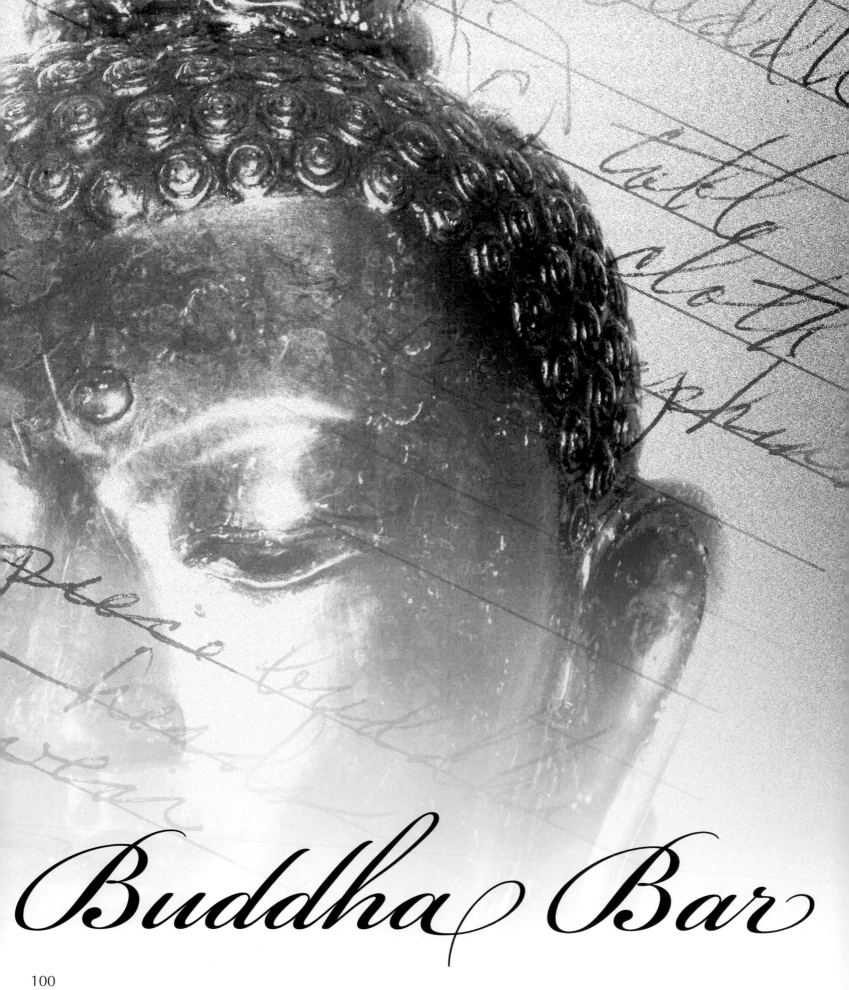

Buddha Bar

My Buddha Bar was inspired by the fabulous Buddha Bar in Paris, whose three-story tall Buddha statue represents the union of all cultures and nations that value peace and harmony and breaking bread together. It's very spiritual to me, so I decided to introduce my own version of Buddha-chic, using rich colors, lush textures, exotic spices, and these great Buddha candles, which I fell in love with. It was an evening of good karma through the sharing of delicious food, treasured friendships, and the appreciation of peace.

-Elaine

EVERYTHING YOU EVER WANTED TO KNOW ABOUT
NAPKIN RINGS BUT WERE AFRAID TO ASK –

buddha-licious napkin rings

Love is in the details, and adding napkin rings is like throwing a kiss
to your guests. When my mother told Amen of Amen Wardy that she
was looking for a Buddha vibe, he showed her these fat, happy Buddha
napkin rings. Amen explains, "A napkin without a napkin ring is like
a woman going out without jewelry." Buddha with his big belly is a
symbol of prosperity in Chinese culture, so if you rub the Buddha belly
you are assured good fortune.

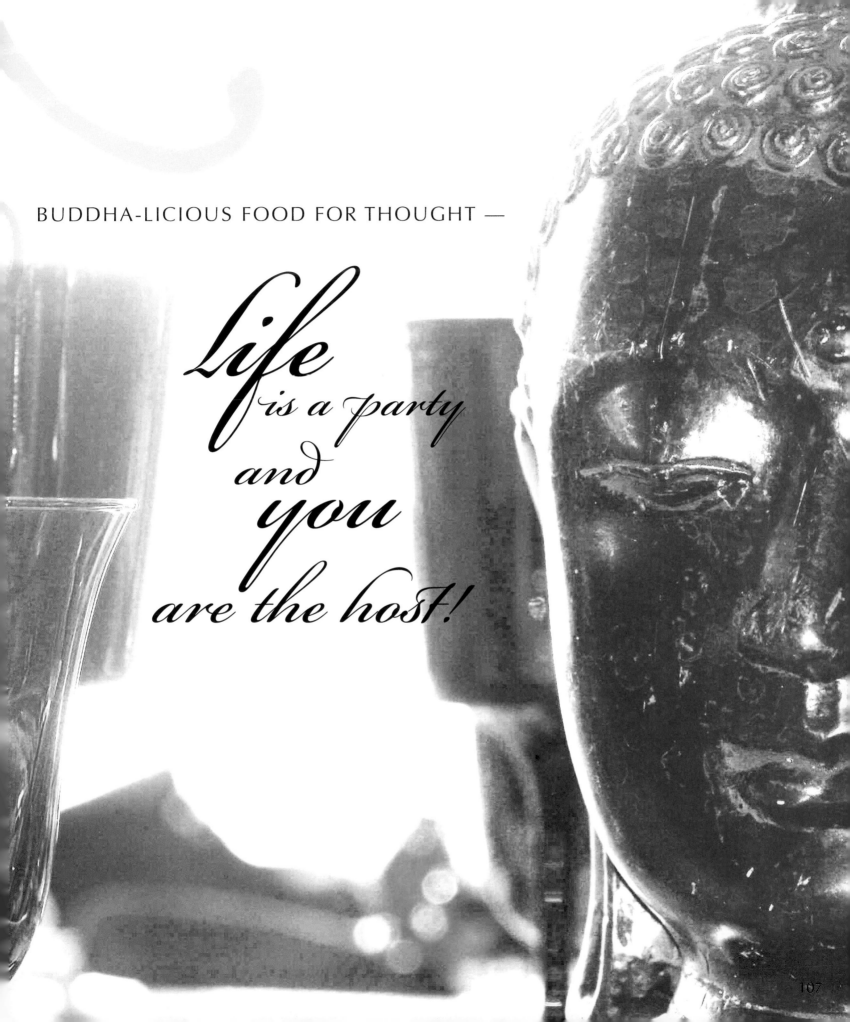

Life is a party and you are the host!

As a child, I loved tales of far away India with its vibrant colors, spices, delicious food, and spiritual traditions. I decided to take a little dramatic license with Elaine's Buddha Bar theme and explore the many cooking styles ranging from the north to the south of India. Climatic conditions and historical influences create each region's diverse outlook on food, although spices always play a huge role in Indian kitchens.

Michael

Menu

Appetizer

Chapati - Unleavened Bread

Puri - Deep-Fried Bread

Poppadums - Flaky Fried Bread

Samosa - Beef Sirloin Stuffed Pastry

Chickpea – Lentil Dip

Red Curry Coconut Shrimps with Mango Chutney

Menu

Curried Coconut Split Pea Soup with Chicken "Tikka" Skewer

Spinach Salad with Curried Cauliflower and Yoghurt Raita Mango Vinaigrette

"Rogan Josh" – Paprika Kashmiri Lamb Stew with Saffron Rice

Dessert

Black Rice Pudding

Special Drink of the Night

Lichee Lassi

Curried Coconut Split Pea Soup with Chicken "Tikka" Skewer

Curried Coconut Split Pea Soup

serves 6

2 tablespoons unsalted butter
1 cup chopped onion
Kosher salt and fresh ground black pepper
1 tablespoon fresh garlic, minced
16 ounces dried green or yellow split peas, picked over and rinsed
8 cups chicken broth
1 cup unsweetened coconut milk
1 teaspoon curry powder
1 teaspoon cumin powder
Pinch of cayenne pepper

Place the butter into a large (4 to 6 quart) saucepan over medium-low heat. Once melted, add the onion and a generous pinch of salt. Sweat for 2 to 3 minutes. Add the garlic and continue to sweat for an additional 1 to 2 minutes, making certain not to allow onions or garlic to brown. Add the peas, curry, cumin powder, and cayenne pepper and sweat for 1-2 minutes. Add the chicken broth, increase heat to high and bring to a boil. Reduce heat to low, cover and cook at a simmer until the peas are tender and not holding their shape any longer, approximately 45 to 50 minutes. Add the coconut milk to the soup and adjust seasoning as needed. Using care and a stick blender, purée the soup until desired consistency. Keep warm and heat up when ready to serve.

Chicken "Tikka" Skewers

1 cup yoghurt
1 tablespoon lemon juice
¼ teaspoon ground cumin
¼ teaspoon ground cinnamon
Pinch cayenne pepper
Kosher salt and fresh black pepper
1 teaspoon fresh ginger, minced
1 teaspoon fresh garlic, minced
3 boneless skinless chicken breasts, cut into bite-size pieces
6 small skewers
Radish sprouts for garnish

In a large bowl, combine yoghurt, lemon juice, cumin, cinnamon, cayenne, black pepper, ginger, garlic, and salt. Stir in chicken, cover, and refrigerate for one hour. Preheat a grill on high. Lightly oil the grill grate. Thread chicken onto skewers and discard the marinade. Grill until juices run clear, about 5 minutes on each side. Ladle the soup in warm bowl. Place one chicken "Tikka" skewer into the bowl and garnish with radish sprouts. Serve immediately.

Spinach Salad with Curried Cauliflower and Yoghurt Raita Mango Vinaigrette

Yoghurt Raita Mango Vinaigrette

serves 6

Raita is a yoghurt based Indian salad. It is refreshing and a great addition to Indian cuisine.

¾ pint plain yoghurt

Kosher salt to taste

Pinch cayenne pepper

Pinch curry powder

1 teaspoon fresh squeezed lemon juice

1 cucumber, washed, peeled, and finely grated

1 tablespoon fresh mint, minced

2 tablespoons mango chutney (grocery store)

Put the yoghurt in a small mixing bowl and beat until smooth and creamy. Season with salt, cayenne, lemon juice, and curry powder. Mix well and fold in the grated cucumber and mint. Set aside and rest to allow the flavors to combine. To make the vinaigrette, add two tablespoons of mango chutney and blend in the food processor until smooth.

Spinach Salad with Curried Cauliflower

15 ounces fresh spinach leaves, rinsed, dried, and torn into bite-size pieces

3 tablespoons olive oil

1 teaspoon ghee (clarified butter)

½ teaspoon cumin powder

½ teaspoon garam masala

¼ teaspoon turmeric powder

Kosher salt and fresh black pepper

1 pound cauliflower florets

1 teaspoon fresh garlic, finely diced

1 medium white onion, peeled, cut in half and then into fine slivers

1 cup almonds, sliced, skin on

Heat up a frying pan or wok over medium-high heat. Add the olive oil, add the cauliflower florets, and sauté for 5-7 minutes until lightly caramelized. Add the garlic and onion to the pan and sauté until the ingredients have browned a bit. Add the ghee, cumin, garam masala, turmeric, and season with salt and black pepper. At the last stir, add in the almonds and toss well. Remove from heat and serve immediately with the salad. Toss the baby spinach leaves with the vinaigrette, season with salt and black pepper if necessary and arrange in the middle of serving plate. Top with the cauliflower mixture and spoon some of the vinaigrette around the salad.

"Rogan Josh" – Paprika Kashmiri Lamb Stew with Saffron Rice

Lamb Stew

serves 6-8

2 (1-inch) chunks fresh ginger, peeled, coarsely chopped

8 cloves garlic, peeled

3½ cups water

10 tablespoons vegetable oil

2½ pounds boned lamb shoulder or leg, cut into 1-inch cubes

10 whole cardamom pods

2 whole bay leaves

6 whole cloves

10 whole black peppercorns

½ stick cinnamon

2 medium red onions, peeled, finely chopped

1 teaspoon coriander powder

2 teaspoons cumin powder

4 teaspoons bright-red paprika powder

1 teaspoon cayenne pepper

Kosher salt, to taste

2 teaspoons tomato purée

¼ teaspoon garam masala

2 cups green beans, trimmed

2 cups red bliss potatoes, peeled, cut into ½-inch cubes

1 tablespoon ghee (clarified butter)

1 teaspoon fresh cilantro, finely chopped

Put the ginger, garlic, and 4 tablespoons of water into an electric blender. Blend well into a smooth paste. Heat 8 tablespoons of oil in a wide, heavy pot over a medium-high flame. Brown meat cubes in several batches and set aside in a bowl. Heat up the remaining oil in a small sauté pan and add the cardamom, bay leaves, cloves, and peppercorns. Stir once and wait until cloves swell and the bay leaves begin to take on color. This takes a few seconds. Place the spices on cheesecloth and make a sachet. Add the onions into the heavy pot, stir and fry for 5 minutes or until the onions turn a medium-brown color. Put in ginger-garlic paste and stir for 30 seconds. Add the coriander, cumin, paprika, cayenne, and season with salt. Stir-fry for another 30 seconds, add the browned meat cubes and the meat juices. Add in the tomato purée. Stir-fry for about 30 seconds until tomato purée is well blended. Stir-fry for another 3-4 minutes. Add the remaining water and bring the contents of the pot to a boil, scraping in all of the browned spices on the sides and bottom of the pot. Cover, turn heat to low and simmer for about 1 hour or until meat is tender. Every 10 minutes give the pot a good stir to prevent burning. Add more water to the pot if needed. When the meat is tender, take off the lid, turn the fire to medium-high and boil off some of the liquid, stirring, until the sauce is thickened.

Meanwhile, boil water in a medium stockpot and season with salt. Make sure it has a salty taste, like ocean water. Add the beans to the boiling water and blanch until tender. Remove the beans with a slotted spoon and cool in an ice bath (ice water.) Add the potatoes to the same water and blanch until tender. Remove from water and cool. Before serving, heat up the ghee in a medium sauté pan, add the potatoes and sauté for 2-3 minutes until caramelized. Add the beans and season with salt and a pinch of garam masala and cilantro. Sprinkle the remaining garam masala over the Rogan Josh just before serving.

Saffron Rice

2 cups basmati rice
1 teaspoon saffron threads
3 tablespoons plus 4 cups boiling water
6 tablespoons ghee (clarified butter)
1 cinnamon stick
4 whole cloves
1 cup finely chopped shallots
Kosher salt to taste
¼ teaspoon cardamom, ground

Place the saffron in a small bowl and cover with 3 tablespoons of boiling water. Soak for 10 minutes. Meanwhile, heat the butter over moderate heat in a large 3- or 4-quart stockpot. Add the cinnamon and cloves and stir well. Add the shallots and sauté for about 5 minutes. Add the rice and stir for about 5 minutes. Pour in the 4 cups of boiling water, salt, and the cardamom. Bring to a boil over high heat. Add the saffron and its soaking water. Stir gently. Cover, reduce heat, and cook for 25 minutes. Fluff and serve hot.

Black Rice Pudding

serves 6

1 cup black rice (often sold as "Forbidden Rice")
¾ cup white glutinous rice
1 cup coconut milk (½ can, shaken very well prior to opening)
4 cups water
1 cup condensed milk
1 stick cinnamon
Pinch kosher salt
2 tablespoons palm sugar syrup (or brown sugar if palm sugar is not available)
1 cup heavy whipping cream, half whipped

Rinse both types of rice thoroughly under running water. Add the rice to a large cooking pot, add the water, cinnamon, and condensed milk and cook together on low heat until rice is soft and most liquid absorbed; about 45 minutes to 1 hour, stirring often. Add the palm sugar syrup and cook until most of the liquid has evaporated. Season with salt and add ¾ cup of coconut milk. The longer you can simmer the rice, the better the result. Remove from heat and keep warm. Whisk the cream to soft peaks and add the remaining ¼ cup of coconut milk and spoon over the black rice pudding. Serve at room temperature.

Birds of Paradise

When the snow starts to melt and the weather gets warmer everyone turns from skiing to hiking, biking, and golfing; so I like to keep the fare lighter and usher in spring with a whimsical wine and cheese party. Along with the tropical fun of colorful parrots and hula dancing candles, I love a grand arrangement of birds of paradise blooms to welcome the approaching Aspen summer. After all, when you are spending the spring in Aspen, how can you help but feel that you are living in paradise.

-Elaine

It's weeks before

the first **Thursdays with Mom & Michael** dinner, and my mother is lost inside the front hall closet. Like an enchanted armoire, she is enveloped by her cherished collectibles from travels around the world and shops in downtown Aspen. The sounds of bubble wrap popping and tissue paper rustling can be heard, then suddenly my mom emerges triumphant, her arms full of beautiful platters and candelabras and crystal goblets and she declares, ***"Okay, I think I've got enough to start my Birds of Paradise party!"***

For two years I lived in the Cayman Islands and experienced a tropical paradise with fresh fish, fresh vegetables, and fresh fruit — you could pick right off the tree. I knew Elaine's table setting for this cocktail party would be festive and colorful, so I wanted my menu to reflect the rainbow of colors I experienced during my time in the Caribbean.

Michael

Menu

Cheese Board

Mt. Tam Cheese, Windsor Blue Cheese, Wisconsin Sharp Cheddar

Organic Wheat Crackers, Rye Berry Jam

Appetizers

Boar's Head Prosciutto Ham Sliced-to-Order

Watermelon-Prosciutto Mint Balls

Southern Style Rice Salad with Black Beans and Sweet Corn

in a Key Lime Vinaigrette

Poached Key West Shrimps in Basil Pesto with Homemade Cocktail Sauce

Jerk-Style Spiced Free Range Chicken Thighs and Wings with Mango Peach Chutney

Caribbean Free Range Chicken and Black Angus Beef Skewers

with Spicy Mayonnaise Dip

Blue Lump Crab and Roasted Sweet Corn Fritters with Creole Sauce

Grilled Vegetables in Balsamic and Fresh Basil

Barbecue Pulled Pork Sandwich on Sesame Bun and Romaine Hearts

Roma Tomato-Papaya-Onion Salad in a Poppy Seed Vinaigrette

Smoked Salmon, Pastrami Salmon, and Gravlax with Lemon Dill Sour Cream

Red and Yellow Belgium Endive with Rock Shrimp and Avocado Dip

Dessert

Mini Profiteroles Filled with Creme Patisserie and Coconut Cream

Special Drink of the Night

Homemade Refreshing Orange Sangria

Southern Style Rice Salad with Black Beans and Sweet Corn in a Key Lime Vinaigrette

Rice Salad

serves 6-8

2 cloves garlic, minced
1 medium red onion, chopped
2 ears corn
1½ cups water
2 teaspoons ground cumin
1 teaspoon ground coriander
Kosher salt and fresh ground black pepper
⅔ cup long-grain rice
1½ cups drained, canned black beans
1 cup fresh tomatoes, chopped
1 cup roasted red bell peppers
⅓ cup fresh cilantro leaves, chopped

Mince garlic and finely chop enough onion to measure 1 cup. Cut enough kernels from the cob to measure 1½ cups. In a small heavy saucepan with a tight-fitting lid, bring water to a boil with garlic, onion, cumin, and coriander. Season with salt and pepper. Stir in rice and cook, covered, over low heat 15 minutes. Stir in corn and cook covered, 3 minutes, or until water is absorbed and rice is just tender. Fluff mixture with a fork and transfer to a large bowl to cool completely. Rinse and drain black beans. Stir cilantro, tomatoes, and roasted peppers with beans, and season with salt and pepper. Add some of the vinaigrette and toss well.

Key Lime Vinaigrette

¼ cup fresh key lime juice or regular lime juice
2 tablespoons rice wine vinegar
1 tablespoon honey
1 tablespoon cumin seeds, lightly toasted
¼ cup grape seed oil
¼ cup walnut oil
Salt and fresh ground black pepper

Whisk together the lime juice, vinegar, honey, cumin, and cilantro in a medium bowl. Gradually whisk in the oils until emulsified. Season with salt and pepper, to taste. Do not use a blender to make this vinaigrette.

Poached Key West Shrimp in Basil Pesto with Homemade Cocktail Sauce

Poached Shrimp

serves 6

5 pounds shrimp, raw peeled and deveined
4 lemons cut in half, reserve 2 lemons for garnish, cut in quarters
2 cups white wine
1 thyme sprig
2 tablespoon pickling spice
Kosher salt and fresh ground black pepper
Ice water (to shock the shrimp)

In a large pot, bring enough water to cover the shrimp to a boil. Add lemons, white wine, thyme, and pickling spice. Reduce heat and simmer for 10 minutes. Strain through a fine sieve. Add the liquid back to the pot, season with salt and black pepper, and bring back to a boil. Add the shrimp, and as they reach a boil, remove from heat. Strain the water and plunge the shrimp into the ice water to stop it from cooking. Allow shrimp to chill for about 10 minutes and after shrimp is cooled, strain the water and toss them with the pesto. Season with salt and pepper to taste.

Basil Pesto

2 cups basil leaves
1 tablespoon toasted pine nuts
1 cup + 1 teaspoon extra-virgin olive oil
1 teaspoon fresh garlic, finely chopped
Kosher salt and fresh ground black pepper

In a medium saucepan, heat 1 teaspoon olive oil over medium heat, add the garlic and sauté for about 1 minute until slightly brown. Add all ingredients in a food processor, season with salt and pepper, and pulse a few times to blend the pesto. Do not blend until completely smooth, leave it a little rough.

Homemade Cocktail Sauce

½ cup sweet chili sauce (Asian section of grocery)
½ cup ketchup
2 tablespoons fresh lime juice (about 1 small lime)
1 to 2 tablespoons horseradish sauce
Dash Worcestershire sauce
Dash green Tabasco sauce
Few drops hot sauce
Kosher salt and fresh ground black pepper to taste

Place all ingredients in a small mixing bowl and whisk to combine.

Roma Tomato-Papaya-Onion Salad in a Poppy Seed Vinaigrette

Salad

serves 6

1 fresh papaya, cut into cubes
6 fresh Roma tomatoes, cut into wedges
1 medium red onion, halved and sliced

Combine papaya cubes, tomato wedges, and red onions. Add the vinaigrette to the salad mixture; toss lightly.

Poppy Seed Vinaigrette

1 teaspoon honey
½ teaspoon Dijon mustard
½ teaspoon paprika powder
¼ teaspoon garlic powder
½ teaspoon poppy seeds
Dash green Tabasco sauce
¼ cup fresh orange juice
¼ cup mayonnaise
Kosher salt and fresh ground black pepper to taste

Combine all ingredients in a jar, shake well and season with salt and fresh ground black pepper to taste. This recipe works with fruit salad as well.

SMUGGLER
CONSOLIDATED MINES COMPAN

AUTHORIZED PERSONS ONLY. ALL OT
KEEP OUT TRESPASSERS WHO SURVIVE
BE DILIGENTLY PROSECUTED. THIS INCL
ANY GOVT. EMPLOYEE.
MINE OFFICE-925-2049

The Black &
White Party

Ever since the days of Truman Capote's famous bash, black and white parties have been a crowd pleaser. My homage to this timeless party classic is mystical and chic. Everyone gets a chance to dress up in their black and white finest. Michael and I thought this dinner should have a champagne flavor with caviar and blinis, so I did a more formal table setting that made the room look like an elegant nightclub that Truman would have adored!

-Elaine

the *finishing* **touches**

Once the chinaware, crystal, and linens have been chosen, my mom sets to work on her favorite accent element — the centerpiece. These centerpieces are the crowning glory of her table, and when it comes to working with flowers, the more inventive the vase or container, the better. If unexpected elements like fruit, pine cones, twigs, and Christmas ornaments are used, it adds a truly dramatic touch. For The Black and White Party, my mother decided on shocking red poppy candles that Becky at Chequers thought would be illuminating, and she was right. The dashes of cherry red put spark to the black and white color scheme, which made for an exquisite table. We know how special we are and that it is going to be a very memorable night when my mother adds her unique finishing touches.

Aspen is a jeans town, but every once in awhile we like to get dressed up. When Elaine throws a black and white formal party I get a chance to shine with a truly exclusive menu with only the finest and freshest ingredients. The Black & White Party started with caviar that is black and sour cream that is white, Foie Gras was added, and the menu continued on from there. A black & white tabletop setting inspires me to prepare a special menu with only the very best gourmet ingredients for this formal occasion.

Michael

153

Menu

Appetizers

Osetra Caviar on Russian Buckwheat Blinis, Mini Baked Fingerling Potatoes,
and Potato Rosti (Latkes) with Chive Sour Cream

Smoked Trout and Edible Flowers

Main

Pan-Seared Sturgeon with Fennel Purée and Red Beet Reduction

Lemon Risotto Cake with Caramelized Squash, Artichokes,

Snow Peas, and Butternut Squash Sauce

"Duck Four Ways" - Terrine of Foie Gras with Apple-Shallot Jam,

Foie Gras, Pan-Seared Duck Breast with Huckleberry Sauce,

Slow Braised Duck Confit

Dessert

White Chocolate Bavarian Cream with Australian Rye Berries

Special Drink of the Night

French Martini

Osetra Caviar on Mini Baked Fingerling Potatoes with Chive Sour Cream

Mini Baked Fingerling Potatoes
makes 24

12 fingerling potatoes, if available use different kinds
1 cup vegetable oil, for deep frying
¼ cup sour cream
1 tablespoon fresh chives, finely minced
1 teaspoon fresh chives, cut ½-inch long for garnish
1 teaspoon fresh lemon juice
Fresh ground black pepper
1 ounce of osetra caviar

Preheat oven to 375° F. Scrub and dry the potatoes and prick each potato with a skewer. Place the potatoes on a shallow baking dish and bake for about 35 minutes or until cooked, but not over cooked. Remove form the oven and cool for 5 minutes, cut in half lengthwise. Carefully scoop out the flesh, keeping the skin complete. Slice a little of the bottom so that the potatoes will sit upright while serving. Lightly smash the potatoes and mix with the sour cream, chives, lemon juice, and fresh black pepper. Set aside. In a medium sauce pan, heat the oil until hot and fry the potatoes until they turn golden brown. Remove with slotted spoon and drain well on paper towels. Put a teaspoon of the potato sour cream mixture into the potato, top with caviar, and garnish with chive. Serve immediately because the potato may turn soggy.

Chive Sour Cream
¾ cup sour cream
3 tablespoons fresh chives, finely minced
Kosher salt and fresh black pepper to taste
1 tablespoon fresh lemon juice

In a small mixing bowl, mix the sour cream and chives together and season with salt and fresh black pepper. Place potatoes on a serving platter, add a teaspoon of sour cream and top with caviar.
Note: *season the sour cream lightly since the caviar is salty.*

Pan-Seared Sturgeon with Fennel Purée and Red Beet Reduction

Sturgeon

serves 6

6 fresh sturgeon filets (2 ounces each)
¼ cup olive oil
4 teaspoons osetra caviar
2 teaspoons fresh red radish, grated
2 teaspoons fresh radish sprouts
1 tablespoon walnut oil

Heat olive oil in a medium-sized skillet over medium-high heat. Season the sturgeon with salt and pan-sear, turning once, about 5 to 7 minutes, until cooked through.

Fennel Purée

4 fennel bulbs, stems removed (save a few fennel leaves)
2 leeks, white and light green part, cleaned and minced
½ cup butter (1 stick)
1 tablespoon extra-virgin olive oil
½ cup dry white wine

Cut the fennel into thick ½-inch slices and use a small cutter to make rounds. Heat the olive oil in a medium sauté pan; add the fennel rounds, season with salt and fresh ground black pepper, and sauté on both sides until slightly caramelized. Set aside and keep warm. Melt the butter over medium heat and add the fennel trimmings and leeks, stirring to coat with the butter. Cook for 5 minutes. Add the wine, reduce heat and cook for 30 minutes. Transfer the vegetables to a food processor. Add the reserved fennel greens and process until very smooth. Pass the purée through a fine sieve and adjust seasoning, keep warm.

Red Beet Reduction

2 cups red beet juice
½ teaspoon red wine vinegar

Put the beet juice and red vine vinegar in a small, heavy-bottom saucepan and bring to a boil over medium-high heat. Reduce the heat and simmer for about 25 minutes, or until the juice is reduced to a syrup. Remove from heat. Strain the reduction through a chinois or fine-mesh sieve into a small bowl. Cover and keep warm. To finish the dish, spoon a small amount of fennel purée into the center of serving dish, set the sturgeon filet on top. Ladle the red beet reduction around. Place the fennel round opposite the purée and top with a teaspoon of caviar. Mix the radish sprouts and grated radish with the walnut oil and arrange on the fennel-caviar.

Lemon Risotto Cake with Caramelized Squash, Artichokes, Snow Peas, and Butternut Squash Sauce

Risotto Cake
serves 6

2 tablespoons shallots, finely diced
1 clove garlic, finely diced
1 leek, finely diced
2 tablespoons extra-virgin olive oil
¼ cup dry white wine
2½ cups chicken stock
1 cup uncooked Arborio rice
1½ teaspoons grated lemon zest
2 tablespoons chopped fresh chives
2 tablespoons chopped fresh parsley
¾ cup shaved Parmesan cheese

Heat olive oil in a medium-size saucepan. Add the shallots and garlic and sauté until slightly browned. Add the Arborio rice and stir for 1-2 minutes until the rice is glazed. De-glaze with white wine and reduce. Reduce heat and add chicken stock in small amounts, so that the rice absorbs the liquid and gives the risotto a creamy consistency. Preheat the oven to 400° F. Lightly grease a 9-inch spring-form pan (baking dish). When the rice is tender, remove the pan from the heat and stir in the lemon zest, leek, chives, parsley, and Parmesan cheese. Season with salt and fresh cracked black pepper. Spoon into spring-form pan and spread evenly. Cover the top of the pan with aluminum foil. Bake for 30 to 35 minutes until firm and lightly browned. Remove from oven and keep warm. Run a thin spatula or knife around the outer edge of the pan. Use a medium-size ring mold and cut out 6 round pieces and invert the cake onto a serving plate.

Butternut Squash Sauce
serves 6

2 large butternut squash, about 1½ pounds
2 tablespoons butter
2 shallots, minced
1 sprig thyme leaf
1 cup vegetable broth
2 tablespoons fresh parsley, finely chopped

Cut the butternut squash in half lengthwise to remove the seeds and strings. Peel the skin using a paring knife and cut the squash into small cubes. Set half of the squash cubes aside for the vegetables. Place the butter and shallots in a deep skillet over medium heat. When the shallots begin to color, add the squash and season with salt, fresh ground black pepper, and nutmeg. Sauté a few minutes to lightly caramelize the surface of the cubes. Add the sprig of thyme leaf and vegetable broth. Cover the pan and cook until the squash is tender, about 8 minutes. Remove the sprig of thyme leaf and purée the sauce with an immersion blender until smooth. Add the parsley and keep warm.

Caramelized Vegetables

1 reserved butternut squash (from the butternut squash sauce recipe)
6 canned artichoke bottoms
1 cup snow peas
1 tablespoon butter

Heat the butter in a medium sauté pan on medium heat. Add the butternut squash cubes, season with salt, fresh ground black pepper, and cinnamon; caramelize. Add artichokes and sweet peas, and sauté until the vegetables are slightly caramelized. Place the risotto cake in the center of serving dish, top and garnish with vegetables and spoon the sauce over the top and around. Serve immediately.

Terrine of Foie Gras with Apple-Shallot Jam

Foie Gras
serves 6

1½ teaspoons coarse salt
1 teaspoon sugar
½ teaspoon white pepper
¼ cup cognac
1 Foie Gras, about 1½ pounds, cleaned, veins removed (ask a qualified butcher to prepare the Foie Gras)
1 ceramic terrine mold
6 fresh chervil sprigs
Sea salt
6 slices brioche bread

Season the Foie Gras with the salt, pepper, and sugar. Drizzle half of the cognac in a medium size bowl, add the Foie Gras, and drizzle the remaining cognac over it. Cover with plastic wrap and refrigerate over night. Preheat oven to 275° F. Remove the Foie Gras from the refrigerator and let stand at room temperature for about 15 minutes. Pack the Foie Gras into the terrine mold, pressing it down to remove any air pockets. Wrap the terrine mold in two layers of plastic wrap and place it in a roasting pan or baking dish. Add warm water up to ⅔ of the terrine. Slowly place the terrine in the oven. Cook the terrine in the water bath, until the internal temperature reaches 100°F, for about 30-40 minutes. Meanwhile, cut a piece of cardboard that will fit exactly inside of the mold. Wrap the cardboard in plastic wrap. It can also be done before the terrine gets used. Remove the terrine from the oven and carefully pour off the fat from the top of the terrine, reserving it in a separate container. Place the cardboard on top of the terrine and press gently to remove the air bubbles. Set a brick block, second terrine, or vegetable cans on top to weigh down the Foie Gras. Pour some of the reserved fat over it, just enough to seal the terrine, avoiding any air exposure. Place the terrine in the refrigerator and let sit at least 24 hours before serving. Slice the Foie Gras into 6 pieces and arrange on a serving plate, sprinkle lightly with sea salt. Place a quenelles of the apple-shallot jam on top, garnish with chervil sprig and a slice of brioche.

Apple-Shallot Jam

1 tablespoon butter
½ cup shallots, finely diced
½ cup Fuji apples, finely diced
½ cup red wine
1 sprig fresh thyme, finely chopped
2 tablespoons sugar
Pinch of nutmeg

Melt the butter in a medium saucepan. Add the shallots and sauté until they are translucent. Add the apples and sauté until translucent. Add the wine, thyme, and sugar and cook until the mixture has a syrupy, jam-like consistency. Keep warm.

White Chocolate Bavarian Cream with Australian Rye Berries

Bavarian Cream

makes 6-8

6 ounces Valrhona white chocolate, finely chopped
2 cups heavy cream, divided
1 tablespoon gelatin
¼ cup cold water
4 egg yolks, large
¼ cup + 2 tablespoons sugar
1½ cups whole milk
2 vanilla beans, cut in half length-wise
Porcelain ramekins (small white baking dish)
1½ cups Australian rye berries (specialty food stores)
½ cup heavy cream, half whipped

In a small heatproof bowl, place the chopped white chocolate. Heat ½ cup heavy cream (reserve remainder) in a small saucepan over low heat, stirring occasionally until very hot. Pour about half of the hot cream onto the chocolate. Stir often until melted and smooth. Gradually whisk in remaining cream. Sprinkle gelatin over cold water in small cup; stir to combine. In a medium heatproof bowl, combine egg yolks and sugar. By hand, beat well to combine. In a small, heavy saucepan heat the milk over low heat, stirring often, until very hot. Gradually add hot milk to egg mixture beating constantly. Turn the custard mixture back into the saucepan. Cook over medium heat, stirring constantly, until custard reaches a temperature of 172° F on a candy thermometer. Immediately remove from heat. Add the white chocolate mixture to the cooked custard and stir it in thoroughly. Add the soaked gelatin and stir until the gelatin grains are dissolved. Strain the mixture through a fine strainer into a large metal bowl. Partially fill the larger container with ice and cold water, and set the bowl of white chocolate custard into it. Whisk frequently until the mixture begins to thicken. Scrape the bottom and sides of the bowl. You do NOT want the custard to set at this point, so watch it carefully and remove from ice water. In a chilled medium bowl, beat the reserved 1 cup heavy cream until cream forms a soft shape. Quickly but gently and thoroughly, fold in softly whipped cream. Mixture will be thin at this stage. Pour mixture into ramekins; spread evenly and place ramekins in the refrigerator for at least 4 hours. Loosen Bavarian cream from all sides of mold gently with a plastic knife. Dip ramekins into hot water for a few seconds. Turn serving plate upside down on top of Bavarian cream. Holding plate and ramekin together, invert. Serve with rye berries.

filling the room

When my mother sits down at her desk to plan each party, she thinks about who might provide an interesting mix for the evening and who is in town. Aspenites tend to be world travelers and adventurers so there are plenty of eclectic and diverse folks to invite. The uniqueness of Aspen is that small town quality where everyone is ready for fun. My mom likes to arrange decorative name plates to mix up the men and the women, because a little flirtation never hurt anyone's spirits at a dinner party. For dessert she makes sure the men change places to keep the energy high. Breaking bread together is a way of saying you are my friend and welcome to my home.

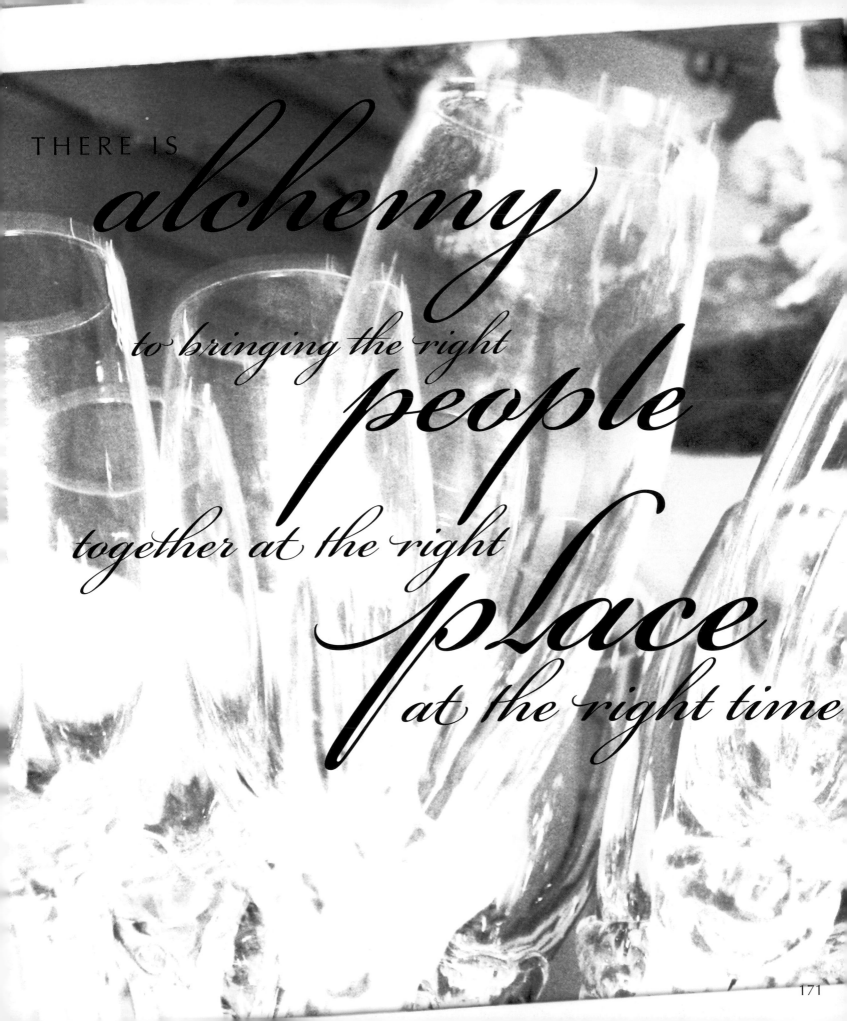

THERE IS *alchemy* to bringing the right *people* together at the right *place* at the right time

Midnight in Morocco

*M*arvin and I took a trip to Morocco that was a once in a lifetime experience. After watching camel races and the sun sink below the horizon on the desert landscape, we were royally wined and dined. I had never been inside such a magnificent tent or sat on such priceless Persian rugs. Midnight at the oasis made such a lasting impression on me that I wanted the final party of the season to reflect this special memory. Although we did not have camels or sand, it was still a magical Arabian night.

-Elaine

to Rent or not to Rent—

THAT IS THE QUESTION

Occasionally, you invent a party theme and in order to pull it off you might need to rent a few fabulous items to give you the ultimate exotic experience. This is what my mother did for her Moroccan party. By adding exotic drapery, tufted stools, glass lanterns, and tenting the ceiling with luscious fabrics, she was able to re-create an Arabian night in her living room.

dazzling bracelets for the ladies

In Morocco, the women wear swathes of colorful silk and sparkly jewelry so my mother thought it would be fun to liven up her table setting with bejeweled bangles. Anything with jewels looks amazing on a Moroccan table. These bracelets came from downtown Aspen, and the ladies enjoyed playing dress up. How fun to be able to take home an exotic parting gift to remember the evening.

the toastmaster raises his glass

"We welcome you as friends and thank you for sharing this evening with us. Some of you are good friends coming in and some of you we will know better as the evening goes on. And some of you will be new friends with each other when you leave. Elaine and I are very thankful and blessed that we can all gather together in an atmosphere of positive feeling and be able to enjoy Aspen and this lifestyle we all work so hard to be a part of. Here's to health and happiness, and we want to thank you for being part of our extended family."

Marvin

Walking through a bazaar in Tangier, Morocco during my work as a chef on a cruise liner, I was amazed by the variety of food and fragrances that greeted me around each corner. The unique combinations of European and Arab influences combined with rich and exotic spices like cinnamon, cumin, coriander, saffron, paprika, and ginger inspire my culinary imagination. This experience is what I wanted to bring to my Moroccan menu.

Michael

Menu

Appetizer

Grilled Lamb Chops with Chermoula Sauce

Artichoke-Spinach Phyllo Triangles with Cumin Spiced Dip

Main

"Harira" - Traditional Red Lentil and Chickpea Soup

Shredded Carrot-Spinach Salad with Orange Wedges in an Orange Vinaigrette

Moroccan Spiced Rubbed Leg of Lamb with Apricot Chutney,

Curry Spiced Couscous and Green Beans with Almonds

On the Table

Chickpea Hummus

"Baba Ganoush" - Roasted Eggplant Spread

Pita Bread Stuffed with Moroccan Spiced Chicken

Roasted Red Pepper Hummus

Dessert

Moroccan Date Pudding with Dried Fruits and Pistachios

Special Drink of the Night

Green Tea with Fresh Mint

Grilled Lamb Chops with Chermoula Sauce

serves 6

6 double bone lamb chops, cut in half
½ tablespoon olive oil
½ teaspoon Hungarian sweet paprika
⅓ cup fresh parsley, finely chopped
1 garlic clove, roasted, minced
2 cups fresh tomatoes, seeded, chopped
⅓ cup fresh cilantro, finely chopped
½ teaspoon ground cumin
½ teaspoon curry powder
Dash green Tabasco sauce
Kosher salt and fresh ground black pepper

Chermoula Sauce

Heat olive oil in a medium-sized saucepan over medium-high heat. Add garlic, cumin, curry, and paprika and sauté until garlic is golden brown. Add tomatoes, cilantro, and parsley and simmer until tomatoes are juicy. Stirring occasionally, season with salt, pepper, and green Tabasco sauce. Transfer to a small bowl and cool.

Grilled Lamb Chops

Heat grill on high. Season lamb chops with salt and pepper and grill on both sides, around 2 minutes each side. Spoon chermoula sauce over the lamb chops and serve immediately.

Shredded Carrot-Spinach Salad in an Orange Vinaigrette

Salad
serves 6

1 pound fresh carrots, peeled & shredded
4 fresh oranges cut into wedges
1 medium red onion, sliced
5 cups fresh spinach leaves, washed and rinsed
¾ cup red radishes, thinly sliced
½ cup fresh cilantro, finely chopped
Grilled pita bread, cut into wedges

Combine carrots, oranges, radishes, and cilantro in a medium-sized salad bowl. Whisk together the olive oil, juices, cinnamon, salt, and black pepper.

Orange Vinaigrette

2 tablespoons fresh lemon juice
2 tablespoons fresh orange juice
1 dash cinnamon powder
3 tablespoons extra-virgin olive oil
Kosher salt and fresh ground black pepper

Pour the vinaigrette over the salad and mix well. Cover and chill or serve immediately. Serve garnished with pita wedges.

Moroccan Spiced Rubbed Leg of Lamb with Apricot Chutney, Curry Spiced Couscous, and Green Beans with Almonds

Moroccan Spiced Rubbed Leg of Lamb

serves 6-8

3 pounds boneless leg of lamb
2 teaspoons turmeric
2 teaspoons cumin
1½ teaspoons coriander
1 teaspoon paprika
½ teaspoon cinnamon
¼ teaspoon ground cloves
1 teaspoon fresh thyme, finely chopped
1 teaspoon fresh rosemary, finely chopped
Kosher salt and fresh ground black pepper
3 tablespoons olive oil
2 medium yellow onions, thinly sliced
3 cloves fresh garlic, finely chopped
1 quart chicken stock
2 tablespoons butter
3 tablespoons pine nuts, toasted
1 teaspoon mild curry powder
3 cups couscous
Apricot chutney (specialty section of grocery)

Combine the 7 spices in a small bowl and add the fresh thyme and rosemary to make a great spice rub for the lamb. Rub the leg of lamb with the spice rub. Shake and evenly coat the lamb in the spices and season with salt and black pepper. Heat a large, deep skillet over medium-high to high heat. Add 3 tablespoons of olive oil and add the lamb to the skillet. Sear the lamb and caramelize the meat all over, 5 to 7 minutes. Add the onions and garlic and cook 5 minutes more. Add 2 cups of chicken stock to the pan and place the lamb into the preheated oven. Cook the lamb at 375° F for about 1-1½ hours until the leg of lamb is medium-rare. Remove from the oven and let rest for 10 minutes. Strain the liquid from the skillet through a fine strainer and set aside. During the last 5 minutes that the lamb has to cook, melt butter and toast pine nuts, then add the curry powder. Add 2 cups chicken stock and bring to a boil. Remove pan from heat, add couscous and cover pan. Let stand 5 minutes. Remove lid and fluff with fork. Serve lamb over couscous in shallow dishes and serve with green beans and apricot chutney on the side.

Green Beans with Almonds

6 cups green beans, trimmed and blanched
½ cup almonds, sliced
1 tablespoon butter
Dash cumin powder
Kosher salt and fresh ground black pepper

In a medium sauté pan heat up the butter, add the beans, and sauté for about 3 minutes. Add the almonds and season with salt, black pepper, and cumin powder.

Pita Bread Stuffed with Moroccan Spiced Chicken

serves 6

Moroccan Spice Mix

1 cinnamon stick, chopped in pieces
1 teaspoon cayenne pepper
1 teaspoon cumin seed
1 teaspoon fennel seed
1 teaspoon coriander seed
1 teaspoon sweet paprika
½ teaspoon turmeric
½ teaspoon mild curry powder
1½ teaspoons kosher salt
1 teaspoon brown sugar

Chicken

1, 3½ pound whole free range chicken
Kosher salt
Freshly ground black pepper
1 fresh lemon, halved
1 fresh orange, halved
2 sprigs fresh thyme
1 sprig fresh rosemary
1 clove garlic
3 tablespoons extra-virgin olive oil
1 cup cooked couscous
½ cup golden raisins

Combine the cinnamon stick, cloves, cayenne, cumin, fennel, coriander, turmeric, curry, and paprika in a dry skillet over low heat and toast for a minute to release the fragrant oils; shake the pan so they don't scorch. In a spice mill, grind the toasted spices together with 1½ teaspoons of kosher salt and brown sugar. Preheat the oven to 400° F. Rinse the chicken with cool water, inside and out, and pat dry with paper towels. Massage the chicken skin with the spice rub. Season the inside of the chicken generously with salt and pepper. Stuff the lemons and orange halves with thyme, rosemary, and garlic in the cavity and place the chicken in a roasting pan fitted with a rack. Fold the wing tips under the bird and tie the legs together with kitchen string. Drizzle the oil over the chicken. Roast the chicken for 1 hour. Check the temperature with an instant-read thermometer into the thickest part of the thigh. If it reads 160° F, it's done. Allow the chicken to rest for 10 minutes so the juices can settle back into the meat. Remove and discard the skin from the chicken. Pull the chicken from the bone and shred the meat with your fingers or with forks. Put the shredded chicken in a large bowl and squeeze the lemon and orange halves that have cooked inside the bird over the meat to moisten. Mix with the cooked couscous and raisins; season to taste. Sprinkle pita bread with olive oil and bake in the oven until warm and crispy. Fill the pita bread with the chicken couscous mixture and serve warm.

Moroccan Date Pudding with Dried Fruits and Pistachios

Whipped Cream Mixture

serves 8

2 cups heavy cream
2 teaspoons vanilla extract
2 teaspoons granulated sugar
½ cup granulated sugar
⅓ cup all-purpose flour
¼ teaspoon kosher salt
2 cups whole milk
3 large egg yolks, beaten
1 teaspoon pure vanilla extract

Whip all of the ingredients of the whipped cream mixture to stiff peaks. Set aside in the refrigerator to keep cool, until making the pudding.

Moroccan Date Pudding

½ cup dried dates, cut in half
½ cup dried figs
¼ cup dried pistachios, roughly cut
¼ cup roasted macadamia nuts, roughly cut
2 tablespoons Grand Marnier
Sprig fresh mint, for garnish
Almond macaroons (grocery store)

In a large heavy saucepan, mix the sugar, flour, and salt; stir in the milk with a whisk. Cook the mixture over moderate heat while stirring constantly until slightly thickened. Slowly stir in approximately ¼ cup of the hot mixture into the beaten egg yolks. Next add the yolks to the balance of the hot mixture and cook, stirring constantly until the mixture is fully thickened to a custard-like consistency and coats a spoon. Remove from heat and stir in the vanilla. Let cool completely and then fold in ½ cup of the whipped cream. Fold in the dates, figs, pistachios, macadamia nuts, and Grand Marnier. Fold in the remaining whipped cream. Fill the custard into a large crystal or trifle bowl and cool in refrigerator until set. Serve cold and garnish with almond macaroons and fresh mint sprig.

THANK YOU
for
sharing

THURSDAYS
WITH MOM
AND MICHAEL

recipe index

acknowledgements

My mother and I are truly grateful to everyone who helped make our dream book come true. First of all, we want to thank our world famous chef, Michael Rueggeberg, who had Thursday nights available. Without Michael and his lovely wife, Christine, the idea for this book would never have been possible, "Your recipes are brilliant and they taste delectable. Michael – you are a shining star!" We are also totally indebted to our brilliant photographer, Karl Wolfgang, who took on this project with passion and dedication. He not only took every photograph, but also created the artistry of every page. Without his tireless efforts to bring our vision to life, our dream book would never have been a reality, "We love you Karl (you have been officially adopted as a Rosenberg)."

On the literary side, we want to thank our New York City writing guru, Beverly West, who helped spin our book in the mother/daughter direction. Your witty words are priceless. Thanks also to long-time family friend, Susan Shapiro, for introducing us to Bev in the first place — you are the best. Thank you to the fabulous Aspen folks who have contributed to this project: to Amen and Bob of Amen Wardy we want to say, "You are a joy to know and a host's secret weapon and we love you too." To Becky Dumeresque, owner of Chequers, "You are very gifted, and it's scary how much you and my mom think alike. We consider you family." To Janet O'Grady, editor of Aspen Magazine, a special thanks for suggesting your top photographer, Karl, and slipping us his phone number — meeting and working with him has been the highlight of our book. Thanks to the Cheese Shop, The Aspen Branch Floral Arts, Noori's Collection, Aspen City Market, Brian at Clark's Market, and Boar's Head. We also want to thank the Aspen Writers' Foundation and Executive Director, Lisa Consiglio, for providing a playground for budding writers, such as myself, to learn and grow. To the dynamic team at words, pictures, colours in Basalt, headed by owner, Kelly Alford and production designer, Sharon Newsom — we are grateful for all of your hard work and your fabulous fonts. My sincere thanks to Elizabeth Winick and Rebecca Strauss, my agents at McIntosh & Otis, for their encouragement and support. And to women we admire, Carolyne Roehm and Laura Werlin, who were gracious enough to offer their expert testimonials. Your support means the world to us and to Michael. And finally, a heartfelt thanks to Evelyn Lauder, for her beautiful introduction, "We are honored to be able to contribute to the important work that your foundation is doing to prevent breast cancer."

A party is just a party without family and friends to share the celebration, so we would like to thank the following party animals and loves of our lives; Susan, David W., Zach, Drew, David R., Gina, Max, Oliver, Will, and Barry.

*And if it wasn't for our Aspen Family there would not be any **Thursdays with Mom & Michael** so thank you to Inez and Stephen Allen, Lois and Dave Alvarez, Elaine and Bob Blatt, Ester and Jerry Bovino, Elaine and Harris Cahn, Dexter and Dennis Cirillo, Brenda and Lester Crain, Lorraine and Alex Dell, Becky and Michael Dumeresque, Nina and David Eisenstat, Shelly Ellard, Jill and Harry Feldman, Fran and Fred Felzer, Sistie Fischer and Doug Allen, Barbara and Aaron Fleck, Marilyn and Mel Gallant, Louise and David Gitlitz, Doug Gilstrap, Amy and Barry Gordon, Marilyn and Dean Greenberg, Marcie and Howard Gross, Carolyn and Ken Hamlet, Judy and Wayne Harris, Barbara and Jim Hilliard, Eveline Hoffman and Joel Strumph, Carolyn and Glenn Jeffers, Sylvia and Dick Kaufman, Ellen and Fred Kucker, Ethel and Allen Levantin, Francine and Tag Liebel, Karen and Courtney Lord, Tam and Jim Martin, Robby and John Michelman, Lynda and Gary Nathanson, Jeanette Oldenberg, Jade and Clint Philips, Sally and Dale Potvin, Robyn and Dale Rands, Judy and Jim Rifkin, Marilyn and Chuck Rivkin, Debbie and Michael Rose, Judy and Gary Rubin, Hope and Paul Rudnick, Diane and Tony Rutger, Luky Seymour, Judie and Gene Seymour, Nancy and Barry Shapiro, Jane and Larry Sherman, Diana Stein, Melanie Sturm and Marc Zachary, Amen Wardy and Bob Hightower, Frankie and Skip Welfeld, Judy and Alan Wigood.*

The most important thank you goes to Marvin Rosenberg for being host extraordinaire and toastmaster, and for his generous spirit and always encouraging us to follow our bliss, "As long as you girls are having fun." And fun we did have and we hope you enjoy our book as much as we loved creating it.